CARDINAL MINDSZENTY

THE STORY OF A
MODERN MARTYR

BY

BELA FABIAN

NEW YORK
CHARLES SCRIBNER'S SONS
1949

COPYRIGHT, 1949, BY
CHARLES SCRIBNER'S SONS

Printed in the United States of America

All rights reserved. No part of this book may be reproduced in any form without the permission of Charles Scribner's Sons

A

I dedicate my book to all those heroic men and women who through their courage and self-sacrifice saved the lives of the Jews of Budapest.

CONTENTS

Author's Preface		1
CHAPTER		
I	The Child	11
II	The Student	19
III	The Young Priest	27
IV	The Scourge of Bela Kun	32
V	After the Commune	45
VI	"The Pope of Zala"	50
VII	"This Man Fears Only God"	66
VIII	A Bull Is Sold	72
IX	Arrow-Cross and Swastika	82
X	The Prisoner of Sopron-Kohida	95
XI	Hammer and Sickle	102
XII	The Symbolism of a Blood-Red Hat	108
XIII	The Tightening of the Net	127
XIV	"Now Men Are Needed"	144
XV	Time Runs Out	158
XVI	The Iron Hand in the Rubber Glove	169
XVII	The Trial	178
XVIII	The Picture	199
Index		205

Cardinal Mindszenty

Author's Preface

THIS is a book about Joseph Cardinal Mindszenty, Prince Primate of Hungary, a modern Christian martyr in the fight against barbarism. It has been my wish from the beginning of its preparation to emphasize the story of his life, his fight against the dark forces which have overwhelmed Hungary and much of Europe, and the significance of his story to a world faced with the greatest crisis in human history. I have no desire to write about myself. Anything which I say in this preface or later in the book, I say only to make his story more fully understandable to the English-speaking reader.

Yet only by telling some of the facts concerning my own life can I explain fully how I came to understand the greatness of the man, and on what sound bases my sympathy and admiration for Mindszenty stand.

I was born in 1889, in the community of Tallya, a center of the famous Tokay wine-growing district of Hungary. My parents were God-fearing, religious Jews and, true to my heritage and early religious training, I have always remained a member of the Jewish congregation. My undying admiration for Joseph Mindszenty is not a product of Catholic partisanship. That partisanship which we have always shared is not affected by any details of theological or ritualistic differences. It is based solidly upon the love of human freedom and honesty which we have both held throughout our lives. It is rooted deeply in our common fight against the forces of reaction and darkness, which, in wave after wave, have assailed our sorrowing country during these years in which we both have lived. Regardless of the fact that Mindszenty is a Prince Primate of the Catholic Church and I am a Jew, whose life has been spent in politics, we have always worshipped the same God.

After I received my L.L.D. degree I became a law clerk in the office of Dr. William Vazsony, an outstanding legal authority, leader of the Democratic Party of Hungary, and later Minister of Justice.

But my law work was early interrupted by the first World War. As an officer in the Hungarian army I was taken prisoner by the Russians in the spring of 1915 and confined in a camp at Tashkent. There I learned the Russian language and, though I was well treated as an officer, first became acquainted with the brutality of which Russian prison camp officials were capable. I shuddered at their treatment of common, rank-and-file war prisoners who were driven almost beyond bearing as slave laborers while being fed on starvation diets. I made my first protests to Russian authorities at this time and as a result was transferred to a punitive camp at Krasnaya Ryechka in eastern Siberia, four hundred miles north of Vladivostok.

Most prisoners of war in Russia looked forward to the Russian Revolution as a great democratic victory which would at last bring the huge eastern empire into harmony and cooperation with Western democratic civilization. Soon we learned what the Communist victory really meant and saw growing before our eyes a power which was the exact antithesis of democracy.

AUTHOR'S PREFACE

Early in 1918, I escaped from Krasnaya Ryechka, and, constantly in hiding, struggled through five thousand miles torn by civil war, mass brutality and destruction, to Leningrad. While the treaty of peace was under discussion at Brest Litovsk, Leningrad was in the grip of a cruel fratricidal war launched by the Communists against the followers of all political movements other than Communism, chief among whom were the democrats and progressives. Since non-Communist news sources were soon suppressed, the only way to gain accurate information was through observation and personal contact. This I managed by edging my way into the galleries of Soviet meetings and other public assemblies and listening in cafes to democratic journalists who functioned as "living newspapers."

Finally reaching Hungary I returned to Budapest appalled by the significance of Russian Communism to the free world. I was further frightened when I found that in Hungary, as elsewhere in the world at that time, many of the most progressive men of good will believed that the Bolshevik victory represented a most encouraging step forward in the organic evolution of democracy. Convinced that the exact opposite was the truth, I tried to disillusion them through lectures and public articles, telling them what Russian Communism was really like, and through three books, *Russia's Decay Under Bolshevik Rule, Russian Inferno*, and *Petrograd*. These publications met with cold incredulity on the part of middle-class intellectuals and made me the target of venomous attacks from the extreme left. As a result I was one of the first to be arrested and placed in solitary confinement at the personal order of Bela Kun, when in 1919 the supreme power in Hungary was seized by this earliest representative of Communist expansion.

After the collapse of this short-lived dictatorship, the other extreme, the white terror regime, for a little while held the upper hand in Hungary. It took vengeance on many of the guilty, and subjected thousands of innocent victims as well to suffering, and not a few to death. Since my fight up to now had not been merely anti-Communist but had been directed against all forms of totalitarianism I opposed this regime as uncompromisingly as I had that of Bela Kun. Seeing in this kind of counter-revolution as great a danger as that which existed in Communist dictatorship, I published three further books, *The Russian Pattern, Methods, Devices and Consequences of Bolshevik World Propaganda,* and *The History of the Russian Counter-Revolution.* This fight made me the target of the same kind of hatred which had been directed against me by the Communists and, following an anachronistic, and perhaps deplorable, Hungarian custom, I was forced to fight over a score of duels with swords and pistols in defense of my principles.

As a result of this democratic record I was elected executive member of the Budapest Municipal Council in 1920, and in 1922 was sent to the Hungarian Parliament by the Budapest suburban district on the Independent Democratic ticket. For seventeen consecutive years I represented my party thus and, in 1928, I was made president of it.

Throughout the period which ended with the engulfment of Europe by Nazism I continued my fight in and out of Parliament against both huge centers of totalitarian aggression, Germany and Russia. In the beginning my

AUTHOR'S PREFACE

warnings about the menace of Nazism were received with the same mocking incredulity as had been my earlier prophecies about the Bolshevik danger. But the Nazis themselves took me more seriously. When the German hordes invaded Austria and Czechoslovakia one of the magazines in Budapest published on its front page a caricature in which I was represented as a dwarf battling a tornado. Under it was the legend "Little Man What Now?"

When the Germans invaded Hungary in 1944, all Hungarian democratic politicians were immediately arrested. I was the only one who was not deported to Mauthausen, Austria. At the special request of my greatest political enemy, the Hungarian Nazi Under-secretary of Home Affairs, I was sent to Auschwitz with its mass-devouring gas chambers.

By what still seems to me to be a miracle I was not one of the thousands of gas victims, and as a prisoner, became part of a group which organized secret radio listening posts within the prison camp. One of the tasks at which we were made to work was the dismantling and reprocessing of parts of American planes which had been shot down by the Germans. Secreting radio parts, bit by bit, from these, the prisoners constructed several secret radios and set up concealed listening posts at which we received news from the BBC and the Voice of America. In order to keep up the spirits of the rest of the prisoners a grape-vine news-service repeated throughout the camp what was heard at the listening posts.

Occasionally the Germans would discover one of these radios and promptly hang those who worked at the secret station or spread the news received. In Auschwitz life was cheap, but the hunger for news was so persistent that though on one day a radio team would be hanged, the very next day a new radio would be working.

Later I was transferred, first to Oranienburg, then to Sachsenhausen, and then to Ohrdruf. From Ohrdruf I escaped in March 1945 with three comrades, hid for ten days in the forest of Thuringia and finally succeeded in creeping through the German lines to find refuge with Patton's American Army. I was given wonderful care and interviewed by American newspapermen to whom I gave the first eye-witness accounts of what was really happening in German concentration camps.

Thus I know at first hand the evils against which Mindszenty fought.

I first met him when he was Joseph Pehm, the Abbe of Zalaegerszeg, leading the fight against Nazism in western Hungary. It was near the end of the thirties when the Arrow-Cross Party, supported by Germany, was exercising strong pressure on the political life of Hungary, and the Hungarian Nazi press was openly announcing that the Arrow-Cross would soon take over power. Their persecution of the Jews was already underway. There were frequent references in their publications to Regent Horthy's wife whom they nicknamed "Rebecca" in abuse of her Jewish origin.

In view of my own stand against Nazism and anti-Semitism and my position in Parliament, I was constantly being asked for help by those who were persecuted. There were frequent complaints about Bela Teleki, the pro-Nazi prefect of Zala County, Mindszenty's county. Having heard a great deal about the Abbe, knowing his stand

AUTHOR'S PREFACE

against anti-Semitism, and his growing influence, I wanted to ask his help along with that of a near relative of the prefect, Joseph Teleki. I talked to them together. Mindszenty at once told me that he had already tried several times to change the Prefect's anti-Jewish attitude but without result.

"Yet one must never give up hope," he said. "Here one of the most deadly dangers threatens the country. The persecution of Jews recalls the early persecution of Christians. Those who threaten any religion threaten all religions."

"I am absolutely of the same opinion," Count Teleki said. "Today it is the Jews, tomorrow it will be you and me."

The Count who had also tried earlier to influence the Prefect, promised to speak to him again, though with little hope.

"Good," Mindszenty said. "It is now that we need men." Throughout the years that followed he was quoted over and over as using these words in times of crisis.

I heard them quoted again when, having escaped the German concentration camp, I was a lonely refugee in Paris, hoping against hope for the release of my wife, who lived for three months during the siege of Budapest in a cellar with our dearly loved dog. The Russians refused through long years to grant her permission to leave the country. (My hope was eventually realized, however, and both are with me today.)

At that time a bitter campaign of villainy against Mindszenty was beginning in Hungary. I read the attacks in Hungarian and foreign newspapers and I knew beyond doubt what his fate would be if he stayed in Hungary. I was sure that the Communist regime would be happy to get rid of him without, through liquidation, bringing the censure of the civilized world down on their heads, and that they would gladly help him to leave the country. Why then did he not go while there was still time? Was it merely that he did not want to abandon his people? Was it that he was unwilling to become the object of criticism? I even argued with him in my mind. "Out here," I said, "you could be free to help prepare for the resurrection of your country."

As I was thinking about this a political friend of mine, who had been very close to Cardinal Mindszenty in the fight against both the Nazis and the Russians, escaped from Hungary and came to Paris. With tears he told me that everything dear to him was in ruins. Before my face he wept with sorrow and longing for all that was irretrievably lost to him—his family, his house, his garden, the green woods of his beloved Hungary.

I had lost all of these things too. I understood his grief. I had no desire to argue with him. Rather I wanted to comfort him in his self accusation for having run away.

"But you are fortunate to be here," I said. "You'd be in prison if you were at home."

"I know," he replied. "I'd be at 60 Andrassy Street in the hands of the Secret Police."

"Exactly," I answered. "And before you were killed you would be forced to betray all of your friends. They would make you give them the names of everyone you love. No one can hold out against their methods of torture."

"I know that, too," he answered. "That was why I went

away. I saw that the fight could not be continued. I was unwilling to join them and yet I was afraid of 60 Andrassy Street—afraid of death to be sure, but even more afraid that they would make me betray my friends."

"Then why do you reproach yourself?" I asked. "You had no choice. There was no other way."

"I keep hearing the words of my advisor," he answered, "urging me to stay."

"And who was he?"

"Cardinal Mindszenty. Before I left I asked him for an audience. He greeted me with the warmest friendliness. Then I told him that I considered my situation at home as hopeless and that I was going to try to escape across the frontier. Immediately he became icy. For a long time he was silent. Then he said simply, 'It is now that we need men at home.'"

Only then did I begin to make progress toward the answers to my questions. But even so the answers did not come at once. To be sure, Mindszenty was a man, such a man as Hungary needed in its most bitter crisis. Yet this was not the whole answer. He was a man in a peculiar position, one which placed upon him, according to his own analysis, a peculiar and heavy responsibility, not only before Hungarian Catholics, not only before Catholics of the world, but before all of the world's freedom-loving peoples.

He could have run away and continued from abroad his opposition to Communism and his work for the liberation of Hungary. Instead he chose martyrdom—not merely the martyrdom of death, but a deeper, more bitter sort. He knew that he would be tortured in prison, that his will-power would be paralyzed by drugs and his meager physical strength broken down. He knew that they would degrade the man and the priest in him, and in this degradation he felt that he could show the world as in no other way what product the mills of the Russian police grind out. He knew his own reputation as a strong man. His martyrdom was to be one of the most convincing messages of modern times. It was to say, "This is what happens to a strong man behind the Iron Curtain. In the light of that, what must happen to the weak of the entire world if the march of barbaric Communism is not halted?"

That is the kind of man Mindszenty was. I have written this book in the hope that it will emphasize his message to freedom-loving men of every faith.

BELA FABIAN

New York, May, 1949

I
The Child

HE WAS born Joseph Pehm on the 29th of March 1892. His home was a one story house made of sun-baked brick at Csehimindszent, a little village of the County of Vas in Hungary near the Austrian and Yugoslav borders. Here, in the western part of Hungary, three tremendous influences had swayed the people from the time of their first settlement on the land.

The first was the land itself, which imparted to the peasants who tilled it some of its own strength and kept them as its loyal children, generation after generation, giving them its apples, its grapes, its wine, its wheat, the strength of its spirit, and its abiding sense of security in return for their unremitting and loving toil.

Here the peasants still poured a little of the new wine on the ground or the floor, saying, "To our Mother Earth." Here the priests, in late Spring, dressed in ecclesiastical robes, still walked into the waist-high wheat, to bless the crop. The land was in the blood of the people.

The second influence was an almost inborn knowledge of the tremendous conflict between paganism and Christianity which had raged more violently here, perhaps, than in any other part of Hungary. It is perhaps not surprising that in this land where so strong a spiritual bond existed between the people and the soil paganism died slowly when the holy St. Stephen won for Hungary its status as a Christian state in 1000 A.D.

And then there was war—war with the barbarians, war with the Tartars, war with the Turks, war with the Germans, war like an eternally living beast which throughout all of the centuries of Hungarian history had raged backwards and forwards across the land. The part of the country in which Joseph Pehm, the future Cardinal Mindszenty, was born, was directly in the path which the war beast most frequently travelled, and where he was most valiantly challenged by Hungarian lovers of peace and freedom. Here in the 16th century, in a single county alone, the Turks reduced the Magyar population from fifty-five thousand to five hundred thirty, but they were still fighting.

Nor was their opposition directed against the foreign invader alone. When in the 17th century the Habsburg King Leopold made a shameful peace with the Turks, and began to oppress his own people, it was in this part of the country that the heroes Peter Zrinyi, Count Frangepan, and the Chief Justice Nadasdi all but perfected their plan to lead the Hungarian people to a new dawn of freedom. Though the plot was discovered and all three were beheaded, the spirit which inspired them lived on.

This country of the Pehms had its traditions. It was in love with freedom, with the soil and with the righteousness, as symbolized by the Cross of Christ. It was to these traditions that Joseph Pehm was born.

The name Pehm, his father's name, is German. Three hundred years before, his father's ancestors had come to western Hungary from Germany. They became Hungarians in all but the German name, embracing the Hungarian

THE CHILD 13

love of freedom, tilling the fertile obedient land, renewing their own spirits each spring with the renewal of the soil. Generation after generation the family remained simple tillers of the soil.

Mindszenty's father continued as his ancestors had before him, growing his wheat and his grapes and his apples on a small holding of land, and raising a large family. But also he took an active part in public life. He was for some time mayor of Csehimindszent and was known as the friend of the poor, courageously taking the part of his people against the abuses of higher authority, whether by the government or neighboring squires.

It was a little village. In the village register for 1947 there was the following entry: "Csehimindszent parochia antiqua, anno 1765 restituta. Matriculae ab eodem tempore. In matre 853, augustiniensis 7. Helvetici—, Judaei—." (Csehimindszent, an ancient parish, restored in 1765. Its register dates from the same time. The number of Catholic souls is 853, Lutherans 7, Calvinists— Jews—.)

The dashes after "Helvetici" and "Judaei" mean that there are neither Calvinists nor Jews in Csehimindszent now, but during Mindszenty's boyhood there was one Jewish family in the village. When the Nazis came in 1944 these were sent to the gas chambers at Auschwitz.

His friendship with the children of this family was one of the earliest influences which later made him try to alleviate the tragedy of the Jew. With them he played in the fields, swam together in the brook and skated on its ice in winter. In the summer they hunted birds' nests together, listened to the whistling of the oriole and lay on their backs dreamily watching the clouds drifting across the blue Hungarian sky. But they didn't go to church together.

Puzzled, the boy asked his father about it.

"Why doesn't Sam go to church on Sunday?" he asked.

"They have a different church," his father told him.

"But where is it?"

"They have no church in this village, for they are the only ones of their religion."

The boy's brow furrowed as a profound question disturbed his mind.

"If they have a different church do they have a different God?"

His father laid his hand on the boy's head, carefully seeking words which would reassure him as he pondered the mystery.

"No, my son, there is only one God. They have the same God as we, only we worship somewhat differently. We are Christians and they are Jews."

In later life Joseph Pehm, as curate, as village priest, as bishop, and as Cardinal Mindszenty was the valiant friend of the Jews in Hungary's most tragic era.

There was a tradition of simplicity and humble modesty in his family. Hard-headed, strong, stubborn in their adherence to the principles of freedom and the dignity of the common man, they were little given to self-praise. Even after Joseph had become Cardinal and was known throughout Hungary and beyond, when anyone praised him before his niece she would say, "Yes, but if only you had known his father!"

Joseph's childhood was that of any Hungarian peasant boy. The fields were the scene of his work and of his play.

THE CHILD 15

Here, as soon as he was able to walk, he began, as all Hungarian peasant children do, to help in the accustomed labor, even when he could do no more than to bring his father's tools or his lunch to him. And here he played his games with the other children—his playthings, the waters of the brook and its smooth stones, the flowers of the meadows, and perhaps an occasional rubber ball which he could hit with a long stick. Here, too, with his family, as the wheat fell in orderly rows at harvest time, he learned the old songs of Hungary. One of them which they sang together in those days so happily, he was later to hear in a more tragic time:

> "I started from my lovely land,
> Beloved little Hungary,
> But I stop and look back
> And tears flow from my eyes
> And tears flow from my eyes."

His mother, whom he loved with a devotion which lasted throughout his life, was his constant companion. (His first book was written to her, for her, and about her, when he was twenty-five years old. Its title was *The Mother*.) Before he started school she had begun his education by telling him stories. From her he learned of the holy King Stephen whose right hand (still carried in a casket through Budapest every year on St. Stephen's Day) and whose Holy Crown are Hungary's most sacred treasures. He learned how in 1000 A.D. a special envoy brought the Crown and an apostolic cross from Pope Sylvester II and on Christmas Day, placed it upon Stephen's head, thus conferring upon him the title "King by the Grace of God." He learned how King Stephen had firmly established the tradition of Christian freedom in Hungary, of his working for the peaceful cooperation of Christian peoples, and of his unceasing efforts to spread Christianity by establishing monasteries and schools throughout the land.

He undoubtedly heard in those days, though it would be years before he would be able to understand the words, Stephen's admonition to his son, Prince Imre:

"If you wish the honor of kingship be peace-loving, rule over all without anger, pride, or hatred, but with love, tenderness, humanity. Remember always that each one of us has the same standing. Nothing else exalts a man as does humility, nothing humiliates him more than haughtiness and hatred. Peace-loving monarchs rule. The rest only tyrannize. Be patient toward all, influential and destitute alike."

It is impossible to tell how much wise words may influence children even though they do not completely understand them. In view of Cardinal Mindszenty's later philosophy and the ways in which he expressed it in action, it may be that this beautiful admonition of St. Stephen's was a fundamental part of the formation of his character.

But there were other stories which his mother told him, stories which had been preserved through centuries by the Hungarian folk. Mindszenty spoke little about his childhood but he frequently mentioned two of these stories. One was about a bluebird and a prince, the other about a porridge mountain.

One day while at play (the first story went) the little prince saw a bluebird and tried to catch it, but, though it

THE CHILD

always stayed near him, never vanishing from sight, he could never quite reach it. Sometimes it flew before him and sometimes it walked, always leading him farther and farther from home, over mountains, through valleys, across rivers and swamps, and into thick forests, where he had to struggle through briars and undergrowth to keep it in sight. He was torn by the wind, soaked by the rain, and his face and hands beaten by hail and snow; through spring, summer, autumn and winter, he followed the bluebird, struggling and straining and sweating, learning to know the peoples of the countries through which he traveled. He could never catch the bluebird, happiness, but he became a good king, for through his own sweat and suffering he learned to know the sweat and suffering of the people.

The other story was one which he told often when he was parish priest of Zalaegerszeg. When the teachers of religion who ate at his table grumbled because of their poor fare and the burden of work put upon them, he would tell them the story which his mother had told him about the porridge mountain.

Once upon a time there was a little boy who wanted to find the land of happiness. He left home and started through the great forest which surrounded the village. Soon he came to a cave at the entrance to which a holy hermit sat in peaceful contemplation.

"Where are you going, little man?" the hermit asked

The little boy smiled hopefully at him. "I'm looking for the land of happiness, Grandfather. Can you show me the way?"

The hermit looked at him gravely, his eyes filled with kindness and sorrow.

"Yes, I can tell you." He raised his hand and pointed. "It is over there, but you must go up and down hill many times. After you have passed through seven countries you'll come to a porridge mountain. You cannot go over it or around it, but must eat your way through it. When you have done that you will find the land of happiness, where sausages and hams hang on the trees, where people eat Christmas cakes every day. There are two brooks there. In one, milk flows and in the other honey. There the people dance and sing with joy, and know no sorrow. But you can find it only by eating your way through the porridge mountain and before you come to it you will have worn out your top boots up to the ankles."

When Mindszenty would tell this story to the teachers who worked under him, he would add, "Do your Reverences understand? We are a small country. The way to our porridge mountain is longer than in other happier countries. Our porridge mountain is larger here than in other worlds, which already have the sunshine of happiness in them. We must walk farther, eat more porridge, and fulfill a greater part of our duty, if we want to find a way through our hardships."

II

The Student

DURING that exciting decade of the 1860's when the spirit of freedom seemed to be sweeping through the world, when Russia freed her serfs, and the United States its slaves, Hungary, too, was moved by the surge toward liberty. Knowing that education is the basis of a free life, the Hungarian government in 1868 enacted an educational law exceedingly advanced for its time, which compelled all children of both sexes to attend school between the ages of six and twelve, and enlarged the school system to make it possible to carry out the program.

Thus little Joseph Pehm was born twenty-four years later to a tradition of education. He went through the common grammar school of Csehimindszent with his brothers and sisters and the other children of the village, and as formal education began to stimulate his thought the three most deeply rooted influences of his life began to assert themselves as he tried to decide even in those early years on a career.

Strong within him was his love of the land; the broad sunlit fields, the rhythmic fall of the rows of wheat before the harvesting scythes, the joyous hum of the threshing machine and the peace of the cool, green recesses of the forest were an everlasting part of him.

Would he be a farmer?

But also there was the love of Christian righteousness which he had gained from his mother and his father. There was his realization that his highest authorities were his devout father and mother and his Reverence the Catholic priest, and that the most beautiful and stirring mysteries which he knew were the humming of the church organ, and the holy wonder of the monstrance in which the consecrated host, the very symbol of the living God, accepted his adoration.

Would he be a priest?

But how could the host have remained undesecrated against the onslaughts of invading barbarians or how could the land, itself, have continued to offer its generous fruits to the peaceful Hungarian farmers had it not been for those heroes of the sword and shield who had given their lives throughout Hungary's history in order to preserve their beloved land?

Would he be a soldier?

The first question was answered for him early. The Pehm land was small and there were six children. An older brother had also wanted to study for the priesthood but at the time when he was ready to go beyond the common school the family had no money with which to send him farther, so he had remained at home to cultivate the land. And so, although Joseph was never to lose his love of the soil or the peculiar sense of joy and peace which he could get by working on it occasionally, he relinquished the thought that he might choose farming as a career. There remained then, the question, priest or soldier?

At last his common school education was finished and the day came when a carriage stood before his house wait-

THE STUDENT

ing to take him to a Catholic boarding school in the ancient town of Szombathely. And now for a moment his love for education seemed to vanish before his love for his mother. Putting his arms around her, he buried his face against her and wept. Gently she stroked his head.

"Dear little Joseph," she said, "but you wanted to go to school, didn't you?"

Miserably he nodded his head, but still he sobbed and still he clung to her and finally she had to lead him gently to the carriage herself, her arm around his shoulders urging him on.

It was not long, however, before the fascinating spectacle of the school against the historic background of the town caught his fancy. A part of the ancient Roman province of Pannonia, Szombathely had housed Roman legions at the time of Christ's nativity. The Romans called it Sabaria. Here the emperor Tiberius Claudius established a Roman colony whose people enjoyed all the rights and privileges of Roman citizens. Centuries ago its walls echoed to the marching feet of more than one emperor's bodyguard. Marcus Aurelius spent three years in Pannonia during the second century and often stayed in Sabaria. Here Septimus Severus was proclaimed emperor by his soldiers in the year 193. During the reign of Alexander Severus, Dio Cassius, the famous historian, was the prefect of Sabaria. During Diocletian's persecution of Christians many a staunch follower of the Cross died here. The emperors Constantinus, Vallus, Valentinianus, and Gratianus often dwelt there.

In the fifth century Attila occupied and destroyed the town. Most of its inhabitants fled before the barbarian scourge and laid the foundations of Venice. But after the death of Attila in 453 his followers were driven from Hungary, and Sabaria, together with the surrounding country, continued to be the theater of conflict for the Ostrogoths and Gepidae, the Longobardi, the Avars, the armies of Charlemagne and finally the Magyars, who established modern Hungary. And even after that there were the foreign invaders, the Germans, the Tartars, and the Turks against whom the Magyars had to fight continually to preserve the freedom which they loved.

Nowhere in Hungary is there a spot which could have stimulated more deeply the mind of a boy interested in the struggles and glories of the past. In Szombathely, built on the ruins of ancient Roman Sabaria, Joseph Pehm felt as though he were constantly walking through two and a half thousand years of history. He saw how the conquering strength of barbarians and tyrants eventually vanished before the tenacity of a freedom-loving people. It was a lesson which he never forgot.

And there was the colorful formalism of the monastery itself to set aflame the imagination which warmed his religious zeal. That some of the other students looked down on him because he was a peasant's son, bothered him not at all. Already he had embraced sounder standards by which to appraise his own value. His teachers were monks, canons of the Premonstratensian order, clad in cream colored cassocks, girdled with sky blue cingulums. Taking advantage of their history-soaked location they drew heavily on the past, using its lessons as a basic material in the formation of character. Their teaching was based on the system and knowledge of ancient Rome. Their young-

THE STUDENT 23

est pupils studied Latin and grew on Latin proverbs which sharpened their memories and helped to form their characters. The small boys felt constantly about them the moving shadows of past ages and saw how courage and kindness and wisdom strove against cowardice and tyranny and stupidity.

Joseph was a good student. He learned quickly and kept the meaning of what he learned. As in his earlier childhood he learned through stories told him by his mother, now he listened to the stories of the monks, who loved him and talked to him as fathers. He heard of Mucius Scaevola, who, wishing to set the barbarians an example of Roman courage and endurance, put his hand into a flame and held it there without complaint. Joseph listened and felt himself to be like Mucius. He too would learn to suffer. "We Roman men are like this," he told himself.

He learned of Horatius defending the bridge alone against an overpowering force of the enemy. He was told the story of Regulus who, captured by the Carthaginians, was sent back to Rome to negotiate peace between Rome and Carthage, leaving behind him his pledged word to return to captivity if he failed to influence the Romans to sue for peace. In ringing tones the monks told him how Regulus urged the Romans never to make peace with Carthage and then, keeping his word, returned to sure death at the hands of the Cathaginians.

He learned, too, through the story of Brennus, the barbarian, a lesson which he was often to remember later when Hungary came under the domination first of the Nazis and later of the Communists. The vivid language of his teachers made him see Brennus, commander of the conquering barbarian soldiers, tip with his sword the scale in which the war tribute of the defeated enemy lay, so that it weighed in his favor, and when the Romans complained at the unfairness involved, Brennus said simply, "Vae Victis"—"Woe for the defeated!" He did not need to wait until the Nazis came to learn how little could be expected from a conqueror.

Just before the Christmas holidays, when the first marks of the year were handed to the students in a general assembly, Joseph happened to be watching one of his friends, a Jewish boy, when his certificate was handed to him. He saw the boy's face blanch and then the tears start from his eyes. As the other students left the room the Jewish boy stayed in his place, lonely and disconsolate, and Joseph, the boy who was destined later to become the comforter of many people, stayed too, silent, helpless but unable to leave a friend solitary in his distress.

The master came down to them and asked the Jewish boy why he was crying. The boy handed him his certificate and sobbed, "I have failed in three subjects."

"I know, my son," the master said, "but you'll make them up by Easter."

"But, Father," the boy cried, "I know as much as those who got through."

The master nodded gravely. "That may be, my dear child, but you are a Jew and because the world is as it is, you must know three times as much as the other children in order to get as far as they do. The day will come when you will thank me for having taught you this.

That afternoon Joseph went back to Csehimindszent for the first time since he had left for school. The village was

THE STUDENT

in a holiday mood. At home the Christmas tree stood waiting for him, gay with tiny, colored candles and nuts wrapped in silver paper hanging on its branches. Little presents for everyone lay under the tree. But in the midst of the holiday joyousness, Joseph seemed sad and silent. Finally, his father asked him what was troubling him. He told him the story of the Jewish boy, ending with the cry, "It is unjust that a Jewish boy should have to work three times as hard as a Christian boy."

His father nodded his head gravely. "Yes, my boy, it is unjust. It is the injustice of the world. You will see more and more of it as you grow older. Do not let it become yours."

Back at school he seemed never for a moment to cease asking the reasons for things.

Why did Rome fall before the barbarians?

Why did it have enemies within its own walls, among its own people?

Why was it that for a time it seemed as though Christianity would fall before the Turks?

Why was it that when the Hungarian king defended Christianity alone, the other great Christian kings, Francis I of France and Charles V of Spain fought each other instead of coming to the help of Hungary who fought for the cause of Christ?

He questioned his teachers about these things, always seeking to answer his own most pressing question, would he be priest or soldier? But the monks could not give him satisfactory answers. "History," they said, "does not give an answer to every question. Perhaps historic catastrophes come about because the leaders and the people themselves do not realize soon enough the character of the danger which threatens them."

He must be alert, he decided. He must learn to foresee danger before it came, and learn, too, to help others see it. And more and more he found that he must seek the answers he needed within himself. More and more he became silent and aloof, not given to making friendships easily, characteristics which he showed throughout his life.

And then the answer to his most pressing question came to him in a flash of understanding brought to him again through stories. From his teacher of history he heard how Ugrin, the archbishop of Kalocsa commanded Hungarian troops against the Tartars, how Archbishop Stephan Tomori led the Hungarian army to his and its annihilation against the Turks on the plain of Mohacs in 1526, and how the ringing of Hungarian church bells at noon to this day commemorates the heroism of Janos Kapisztran, a simple Franciscan friar who defended Belgrade against the Moslems.

Priests all of these, priests who loved their native Hungary as did Joseph himself, priests willing to die for her with their swords in hand. Priest or soldier? These had been priests *and* soldiers. And so could he be. And so would he be. His question was answered.

He would be a priest.

III

The Young Priest

HIS decision made, he settled down to the arduous task of preparing for the priesthood at the seminary of the Episcopate of Szombathely. The hours were long and the food meager, but when his fellow students would complain that they were not getting enough to eat, Joseph would say, "St. John nourished himself in the wilderness with locusts and wild honey."

During his summer holidays he worked in the fields with the rest of his family, always carrying a book in his pocket. When they sat down to rest, the others talked while Joseph took out his book and read.

On July 26, 1914, war broke out between Serbia and Austro-Hungary. By the beginning of August the whole of Europe was involved in what we now remember as World War I. All able bodied men of Hungary were called to the national service. Joseph Pehm, along with other students of the Szombathely Seminary, were ordered to serve as Red Cross aides in the five hospitals of the town. Their work was not merely that of nursing, it was also their task to serve the religious needs of the wounded and to administer to their families. Thus, before Joseph was ordained, he was carrying on much of the burden of social work of a full fledged priest and at the same time fulfilling his duties as a student at the school. It was exhausting, body-bending, and heart-breaking work, but those who knew him then say that when one of his fellow seminarists would complain Joseph would say, "Think of our soldiers who are on the battle fields of Russia and know how fortunate we are."

He was ordained June 12, 1915, at Szombathely, at the age of twenty-three. On the 29th of the same month he celebrated his first mass in his native village, Csehimindszent, following an old Hungarian custom according to which every newly ordained priest first celebrates mass in the village of his birth.

It is called "the new mass," and the day on which it is celebrated is always an important feast day. The date for Joseph Pehm's new mass was carefully chosen. June 29th is Peter-Paul's Day, the day on which Hungarian farmers begin to harvest their wheat, a joyous harvest festival day. The choice of this day emphasized the close bond between Mindszenty and his ancestors and the earth.

A new mass is always a great event in western Hungary and attracts people from far and wide. There is a saying there: "It is worth while to go to new mass even from so far away that the soles of new boots are worn through." And Joseph Pehm's new mass attracted more people than anyone there could remember having seen at a similar event.

Sister Emma, now a nun at a New York convent, whose mother was a cousin of Mindszenty's mother, has given me the following account of what happened on that day.

"We lived in a village two miles from Mindszent. We walked there with practically the entire population of our village and all our nearby relations, to be present at Joe's new mass. Mindszent was crowded with people from far

THE YOUNG PRIEST

and wide. There would not have been nearly enough room for them in the village church so the altar was set up in front of it and mass celebrated there. His cousin Joseph Zrinyi, a teacher of religion at Szombathely, opened the ceremony.

" 'My dear fellow priest and brother,' he said, 'you have sworn eternal faith to our Lord Jesus and from now on those laden with sorrow will come to you. Give them consolation. Heal the spirits of those who suffer and encourage the disheartened. Be as a loving father to everyone and send none away from you without encouragement and consolation.'

"This is what Joseph Zrinyi said," Sister Emma reported. "When he finished, the eyes of all who listened were wet with tears. Everybody from the village was there, Catholics, Protestants and the one Jewish family whose children had been the playmates of Joseph Pehm's childhood. A mass like this is not merely an ecclesiastical ceremony, it is also a family feast, the feast of the small family and of the village and all those who belong to it, whether they are Catholics or not.

"When Joe spoke he exhibited at once his talent as a speaker. His speech was direct and easy so that everyone understood him, and yet was eloquent and profound enough to show all that he spoke with authority. There was nothing artificial or condescending in his manner and his words were simple as the fields and the waters of the brook. He spoke to everybody and he spoke as a Catholic priest, the leader of his Catholic people, and yet there was a special intimacy in what he said as though he were speaking especially to those with whom he had grown up, those whom he had learned to know and to love as a child, whether they were Catholics, Protestants or Jews. There was no sense of division between good people in his mind or heart. He wanted each one to be as good as he knew how to be according to his own religion. It was really a beautiful speech."

"But what did he say?" I asked Sister Emma.

"Say?" she answered. "I can't remember his exact words. He said things like that. He said that the people were suffering very much just then. He said that war was raging in the world, that our Lord Jesus' tomb was trembling in the Holy Land, that everybody must do his duty in the village and on the battle field, that all people should help each other. Those who have possessions, he said, have received these from God. If one helps another he doesn't give away his own, he gives only what God has entrusted to him. God made every man alike. The Lord didn't say, 'John you are more than the other so you must carry yourself higher, or you are less so that you must humble yourself.' He said we were all alike. He did not say, 'Thou shalt hate each other.' He said, 'Thou shalt love each other.' He did not say, 'Push that man back because he is a Jew.' The Lord Jesus was a Jew himself, descended from the tribe of King David. Only those who help their brothers can get into heaven, he said, only those who do not push them away but help them."

Here Sister Emma stopped, and I thought how effective the teachings of Mindszenty's father, the simple Hungarian peasant had been in the molding of his life and through him in influencing the thought of the world.

"What happened next, Sister Emma?" I asked.

THE YOUNG PRIEST

"Everybody in the village was very proud that Joe had spoken so wisely and so well. The people all talked his speech over together, the Catholics and the Protestants and the one Jewish family who were all his friends and everywhere you could hear someone saying, 'You'll see! He'll become a bishop!' Aunt Barbara, Joe's mother, wept but she sat there quietly and very proudly. It is true that she never urged Joe to become a priest but it is also true that she was very proud that he had become one and that he showed so clearly at his new mass what a good one he was."

"And then, Sister Emma?"

"Well, we went home to our village on the same day, walking with all of the people who had gone with us, singing and all very happy. The next day I heard that Joe went to the field with his father and brothers to reap the wheat in the new harvest. He could handle the scythe very well and cut tremendous swaths with it. Although he was frail he never seemed to get tired. You see he was used to it."

The new mass and the new harvest! God, and the land, and the people who lived close to the land, were very closely connected in the mind of Joseph Pehm, who was later to become known to the world as Cardinal Mindszenty.

IV
The Scourge of Bela Kun

AT THE end of October 1918, the Austro-Hungarian monarchy collapsed, torn by the waves of revolution which were sweeping through central Europe as a backwash from the tides of war. King Charles IV, already bereft of power, was forced to accept as Premier the bourgeois-socialist Michael Karolyi, who had set up a radical National Council in cooperation with a so-called Soldier's Council. On November 13th the king withdrew from State affairs and three days later the Hungarian Republic was proclaimed.

But from the first the new government was doomed by the march of events. New states were being formed. Czechs, Serbs and Roumanians were busily building armies in order to hold as much territory as they could while the Big Four were deciding how much it was right for each to hold. The Hungarian armies were returning fermenting with the yeast of new political dogmas, in which the seeds of revolution could sprout rapidly.

The Karolyi government was weak, indecisive and helpless. When asked about his policies Karolyi said, "I do not know. I'm being carried by the waves." Should he demobilize the army quickly, thus minimizing the danger of a military revolution, or should he keep it intact to guard the frontiers of Hungary against the threats from Czechoslovakia, Roumania and Yugoslavia? In his indecision he was helpless against the rashness of his Defense

THE SCOURGE OF BELA KUN

Minister Bela Linder who said that "there is no more need for an army. Never again do I want to see another soldier." With the dissolution of the army Hungary was left defenseless.

Karolyi's government was considered a leftist government but soon it became clear that "on the left of the left there is always a left." Hungary was rapidly drifting toward the type of Communism which had brought about the fall of the Russian monarchy in 1917.

The trend toward Communism was greatly strengthened by the return of Hungarian soldiers who had been prisoners in Russia. Among them there had been planted by the Russians a great many trained agitators who were spread throughout Hungary and began at once to exploit the Hungarians' dissatisfaction with the Karolyi government and the general situation. Among these, two highly trained terrorists, Bela Kun and Tibor Szamuelly, took the lead, organizing large scale underground operations financed by Russia and given force by armed detachments of terrorists working in organizations with such names as "The Lenin Boys" and "The Marines."

With frightening and mysterious swiftness they began taking over local governments and eliminating opposition by imprisonment and murder while the Karolyi Government stood by helplessly, acting when it did act, largely in conformance with the demands of the Communists. After four months of weakness and indecision the Government fell and the so-called "Dictatorship of the Proletariat"—actually the Red reign of terror—began.

It was then that Mindszenty's quarrel with Communism began. It was then too that his name, Joseph Pehm, was listed in Russia, among the foreign enemies of Bolshevism, as that of a man who might have to be dealt with when the proper time came. From the beginning of the movement which overthrew the Monarchy, the young priest put the full strength of his youth and religious zeal into clerical and political activities in an attempt to damn the flood which he saw sweeping away the orderly life of his beloved Hungary. At the time of the abdication of King Charles, Pehm was a teacher of religion in the high school at Zalaegerszeg. Here he talked constantly to his students and the people of the village warning them against the Red terror which was threatening the destruction of the country, knowing well that his words would be used against him.

And it was while he was on his way from Zalaegerszeg to visit his Bishop, Janos Mikes, at Szombathely that, on February 9, 1919, the agents of the Red terror against which he had been working took him from the train and placed him under arrest on a charge of counter revolution, imprisoning him in the Bishop's Castle in Szombathely. Eighteen days later, on February 27th, Bishop Mikes was also arrested and placed in a cell in Budapest (I know what his imprisonment was like because I, also an opponent of the Bela Kun regime, was confined in the cell next to his).

After ten days imprisonment, Mindszenty was released. He was asked to promise not to return to Zalaegerszeg but refused and immediately boarded a train to go there. He was once more arrested and taken back to the Bishop's Castle at Szombathely where he was re-imprisoned. When

THE SCOURGE OF BELA KUN

on March 21st the Bela Kun regime took over the national government, Mindszenty was transferred from the Bishop's Castle to police headquarters and taken before a court of law.

There was no trial. He was simply told that with others he was being held as a hostage. "If there is revolutionary activity in western Hungary among those people whom your treasonable propaganda has influenced," they told him, "you will be hanged."

The hostages were a mixed lot made up of Catholics, Protestants and Jews. Their morale was low for they knew how much opposed to the Communist regime the people whom they represented were and they knew how effective were the Red terrorists' methods. Three of them took it upon themselves to keep up the spirits of the rest. One was Istvan Kincs, the parish priest of Koszeg. One was a Jewish lawyer named Rothschild. The other was Mindszenty. They vied with each other to tell amusing stories, to keep the conversation going all the time. Mindszenty, who was known for his reticence and aloofness, suddenly became very talkative. He told them of his childhood. He told them the stories of the Bluebird and the Prince, and of the Porridge Mountain. He recalled little adventures of his school days. He explained to them how difficult it had been for him to make a choice whether to be a farmer, a priest, or a soldier, and how he had settled his conflict. Later his fellow priest Istvan Kincs said that in the talkative, joking young hostage no one would have recognized the stern and silent theological student of Szombathely, or the teacher of Zalaegerszeg. Mindszenty was remembering the admonition given him by Joseph Zrinyi at his new mass to "heal the spirits of those who suffer and encourage the disheartened."

The cell in which the prisoners were housed was crowded and was infested with bed-bugs. There was little sleep there during the night with everyone turning and scratching and turning on the lights in their never-ending war against the vermin. One morning one of the prisoners drew a picture of a gallows on the wall with a rope suspended from it and a noose surrounding a bed-bug which had been crushed there. A little later one of the Communist Commissars walked into the cell and stood for a moment glowering at the drawing on the wall.

"What does that mean?" he asked Mindszenty.

The young priest examined the drawing carefully, cocking his head on one side and then the other.

"It looks like a hanged bed-bug," he said finally, "but you never can tell exactly what it means."

At the laughter of the prisoners the Commissar shouted with rage.

"Take care or you'll all be hanged yourselves."

Mindszenty raised his eyebrows. "Do you think so?" he asked innocently. "After all it can be a warning only to vermin. If we hang one or two of them perhaps the others will be frightened and stop sucking our blood."

There were bad moments in the prison cell as news drifted in of counter-revolutionary activities not far from Szombathely. In several nearby villages when authorities came to take horses for the Red army the peasants resisted with picks and shovels. Others from the village came to their support and there were many deaths. As

THE SCOURGE OF BELA KUN

they heard these reports the hostages trembled for their own lives and Mindszenty was constantly at his task of keeping up their spirits.

Perhaps he proved a greater embarrassment to the authorities as a prisoner than he had been when he was on the outside. At any rate on the 19th of May, having spent three months and ten days in prison, he was released and taken back to Zalaegerszeg. Here Marcus Erdos, president of the Directorate of Zala [1] gave him a lecture on morals and let him go.

The next day Mindszenty was again arrested and brought before Erdos.

"Pehm, you are incorrigible," Erdos said.

"What have I done now?" Mindszenty asked.

"You spent the evening in the company of subversive people," the president charged.

"They are members of my flock," Mindszenty answered.

"They are subversive. You are expelled from Zalaegerszeg. You must leave within two hours."

"For Szombathely?"

"That is perhaps the last place we would permit you to be. You will go to your native village Mindszent where you will report twice every day to the Directorate."

And so Mindszenty returned to his native village where he at once reported to the village Directorate who looked at him a little shamefacedly and apologetically. These five men chosen from the poorer farm laborers had nothing to do with Communism, indeed they were as eager as anyone else for the Red rule to come to an end. They had simply been thrust into their positions as representatives

[1] The Directorate was a five man local government board with dictatorial powers. Zala is the county in which Zalaegerszeg is situated.

of the proletariat by a power stronger than themselves. They greeted Joseph Pehm as a friend, as one whom they had watched grow from childhood, with whom they had gone to school, and with whom they had played along the sparkling brook which ran through the village, as the young priest at whose new mass they had felt very proud, and as one whose parents were among their most respected neighbors.

"Never mind, Joe," they told him. "We shan't trouble you. It won't last forever. You will enjoy being at home and working in the fields with your family."

When Mindszenty joined his family it was in the full sunshine of one of the most beautiful springs which western Hungary had known for years. In the vineyards the strong thrust of the grape sprouts gave promise of a rich vintage. The fields were covered with the bright, joyful green of the new crops. Mindszenty became a peasant again, a farmer—and a priest and soldier. Every weekday and every Sunday he said mass, but before mass he fed the cows and horses, and cleaned the manure from their stables. After mass he slung his coat over his shoulder and together with his dog, who was his constant companion, he went to the fields. Gradually the work on the Pehm farm which had fallen behind during the period of political upheaval and uncertainty was cleared up. Mindszenty mowed grass, hoed Indian corn, and cleaned out the weedy vineyard. At noon he and his brothers had their midday meal together, broiling bacon and onions on long spits over open fires, dripping the fat of the bacon and the juice of the onion on bread, quenching their thirst with clear spring water which they drank from clay jugs.

THE SCOURGE OF BELA KUN

When the day's work was over and his brothers went home to rest, Mindszenty would go into the village, and visit the shop in which the village people congregated, in order to get what news he could in the hope of finding evidence that the Red regime was weakening.

Two newspapers, both organs of the Communist Party, came from Budapest, *The People's Voice* (*Nepszava*) and *The Red Press* (*Voros Ujsag*). Mindszenty read both of these carefully, skillfully interpreting the propaganda, trying to read encouraging news between the lines. When news was brought in by word of mouth of counter-revolutionary activities the people became hopeful, only to have their hopes crushed by despatches in *The People's Voice* and *The Red Press* telling of the execution of counter-revolutionists. Throughout Hungary the beautiful acacia trees became gallows from which hung bitter fruit indeed.

Here, as he had done in prison, Mindszenty tried to keep up the spirits of his people. But when bad news arrived he would go off by himself to restore his own strength in solitude, wandering alone in the woods with his dog, lying on the fresh grass, his hand gently stroking the head of the faithful animal which lay beside him.

The failure of the counter-revolution of June 1919 was an especially bitter blow. It had started so hopefully among a group of cadets in the Ludovica Military Academy (the Hungarian West Point) in cooperation with a group of ironworkers under the leadership of Joseph Haubrich. The first definite news of it came through in the Communist newspapers which told of the many gallows that were being erected on Octogon Square in Budapest for the cadets.

Later, one day when Mindszenty was working in the fields, he heard a group of young men approaching. They were singing as they came:

"I started from my lovely land,
Beloved little Hungary,
But I stop and look back
And tears flow from my eyes
And tears flow from my eyes."

As they came closer Mindszenty called, "Who are you?"
"Students from Debrecen," they said. Debrecen is the Calvinist Rome. For centuries its students and graduates have been known as patriots and fighters for freedom.
"Are you hungry?" Mindszenty asked.
"A student is always hungry," one of them replied.
They sat down in the field and the Pehm family shared their bacon and onions and bread with the students and then when Mindszenty learned that the young men were on their way to Austria he offered to accompany them to the frontier in order to ease their way past a possibly difficult guard. As they walked he learned from them all that he could about counter-revolutionary activities. It was then that he found out how fair had been the hopes for success of the June revolution. The cadets had been well-armed and several Danubian gunboats had been waiting to take part. It had failed apparently only through treacherous betrayal at the last moment.
One of the students said that he was the fourth generation of patriots who had fought for the freedom of Hungary. The name of one of his ancestors who died in the

THE SCOURGE OF BELA KUN 41

struggle for freedom of religion was engraved on a monument near the Calvinist church at Debrecen. Another perished as an exile with Rakoczy in Turkey. Another fled with Kossuth in 1849 and died in the United States.

"It looks like Fate," the student smiled. "I wonder what mine will be."

"It will be to help free your country," Mindszenty said.

The student sighed ruefully. "Arpad put up his tents in the wrong place a thousand years ago. He should have taken his people some place else. He was fooled by the rich soil and the sweet water of this land. He could not see that he had placed us on the cross-roads of eternal war. We must always fight. We must always run away."

Mindszenty walked with the students until daybreak. When they were safely over the frontier he gave them his blessing and they went on, leaving him behind. He stood watching them until they were out of sight and heard them once more take up their song—

"I started from my lovely land,
Beloved little Hungary, . . ."

Turning, he started to walk slowly back to Mindszent, the tears streaming from his eyes.

Refugees came frequently through Csehimindszent to hide in the woods overnight, perhaps, and then to go on to the Austrian border, and Mindszenty always kept in touch with them, bringing them food and clothing, giving them directions for reaching and crossing the frontier, often accompanying them, cheering them and getting such news from them as they had to give. When one such group told him that the execution of the Ludovica cadets had been postponed as a result of intervention by the Italian Colonel Romanelli, he fell to his knees in the forest and offered a prayer of thanks.

Often the refugees would urge him to come with them. It seemed increasingly apparent that the Communist Government could never be overthrown from within Hungary. It did not matter that the whole country was against the Government, including even the factory directorates. A few companies of motorized and armed terrorists were more powerful than an unarmed nation.

"Come with us, your Reverence," the refugees urged. "Help us to prepare Hungary's liberation from beyond its borders where we can be free."

But Mindszenty always shook his head. "I must stay here with my people. Men are needed at home now." Many times during the next twenty years he was to repeat that dictum, sometimes to explain why he stayed in Hungary, sometimes to point out why others should.

While he worked in the fields and during the periods when he walked in the woods with his dog or sat silently in meditation he kept trying to think through the future. What would happen to his nation under Communism? What would happen to religion? What would happen to the world? He felt that the three questions were really one and he could see no hopeful answer to it so long as the Communists held control. How then could they be removed? What form of government should replace them? What part must he as priest-and-soldier play?

Lying in the woods with his dog beside him and copies of *The People's Voice* and *The Red Press* in his hand he

THE SCOURGE OF BELA KUN

read the foreign news. In Germany the Spartacists were undermining the Republicans. In France workers, peasants and soldier's councils were being formed. England and the United States were being torn by strikes and dissension. He knew that much of this news was a product of the propaganda mills of Budapest and Moscow. Yet close as he was to the at least temporary triumph of the Communists in Hungary, he knew that the foundations of pre-war society throughout the world were crumbling. How could Hungary, one of the most troubled spots on earth, be made a bastion against the slow disintegration of religion and decency that seemed to be taking place everywhere?

For many centuries his beloved country had defended European civilization against the menace of the Tartars and the Turks. Now its thousand-year-old dignity was being derided and spit upon, its soil violated, by new tyrants completely devoid of moral sense. Throughout its history religion in Hungary had never been called upon to face a more powerful frontal attack. This was the significant fact. Since 1000 A.D. when the Vatican had placed the Holy Crown on the head of St. Stephen the authority of the Hungarian State had rested in its belief in God. Now that this authority had been overthrown by a power which denied God and the authenticity of faith, what was necessary first of all was to re-establish the front line of religion in the souls of men.

How could this be done? Suppose that the Reds could be overthrown from within or without, what then? How could order be restored with the least sacrifice of human life and moral values? Should the government which followed the fall of the Reds be a Republic or a Kingdom? If the latter, ought a new king to be brought in or should Charles IV who had fled to Switzerland be returned to the throne?

He found his answer in the Holy Crown and the right hand of St. Stephen, Hungary's most holy relic, which generation after generation of Hungarians had recognized as the symbols which held the people together in Christian purpose. He decided against the republic and in favor of the restoration of King Charles.

Now, with his mind made up, he became reticent and silent again, discussing his conclusions with no one. He listened to everyone, the people of the village and the refugees, but he did not tell them what he was thinking. If they asked him when the Red regime would be overthrown he would say, "Perhaps you had better ask my mother, she will tell you the story of the porridge mountain. We are eating our way through our porridge mountain right now."

This always made the people laugh for porridge was the principal food of the Red dictators in Hungary.

"At any rate," they said, "it will be on a feast day. That much we know."

V
After the Commune

RELEASE from Bela Kun and his terrorists came at last, perhaps sooner than Mindszenty had expected. Stubborn and consistent lack of cooperation from the farmers was starving Budapest. The Roumanians and the Czechs, meeting little effective resistance from the poorly disciplined Hungarian Red army, were slicing off for themselves bits of Hungarian territory. On July 31, 1919, Bela Kun, seeing that his case was hopeless, handed over authority to a Socialist government and fled to Vienna.

The news reached Mindszenty two days later. He was hoeing Indian corn when a peasant girl came running excitedly across the fields toward him waving the red, white, and green flag of Hungary. A horseman had just galloped through the village, she said, telling the glad news. As Mindszenty dropped his hoe and started running toward the village he heard the church bells ringing as for a feast day. The people thronged the streets, laughing and crying and some of them singing. They greeted him joyfully. "Didn't we tell you, your Reverence?" they cried. "We said that the Reds would be driven out on a feast day. Hear the bells? Any day on which they were over-thrown would be a day for a feast."

Suddenly an ugly sound rose above the joyous laughter. He heard angry mutterings and imprecations, and saw the crowds shifting to mill about the church before which the president and members of the Directorate were standing apart. One of the women was shouting angrily at them. "Look at the Reds," she cried. "They're the ones!"

Hurriedly Mindszenty pushed his way through the crowd and walked up to the Directorate, shaking hands first with the president and then with the other members. "Come and celebrate with us," he said. "You are honest men. There is no crime on your souls."

It needed only this quick leadership to free the hearts of the people from their misdirected bitterness. Once more the men who had been forced to become members of the Directorate were their friends, and they all rejoiced together, while the church bells voiced their gladness.

Freed now from restraint, Mindszenty went to Zalaegerszeg the next day where he learned that all of the members of the Communist Central Government had fled. Tibor Szamuelly, who had made himself the object of bitter hatred throughout Hungary because of his savagely barbaric abuse of police powers had been intercepted at the Austrian border and beaten to death by a mob. Bela Kun and the other People's Commissars had found refuge in Vienna.

In the evening Mindszenty went to the Catholic club which he found filled with people in an excited and angry mood. They abused the Austrian government for receiving Bela Kun and his murderers. And then Mindszenty heard what he had been fearing for months—ugly, anti-Semitic mutterings based upon the fact that Bela Kun, Szamuelly, and some of the other Commissars were Jews.

The young priest asked for permission to speak and immediately everyone was silent. He was the first to have

AFTER THE COMMUNE 47

been arrested in Zalaegerszeg. He had been the beloved teacher at the high school. His efforts on behalf of refugees were well known. He was the hero of the day.

"My brothers," he said, "let everyone look at his hands. Take care that the blood of innocents does not stain them. For a hundred days you have heard much about collectivism. You have heard of collective responsibility, collective crime, and collective punishment. This is Communist teaching. See that you do not fall into its error yourselves. There is no such thing as collective crime, or collective punishment. Everyone must answer before God and his judges on earth only for the crimes he has himself committed. I hear voices which I do not like, voices uttering collective condemnation just as the Communists do, voices threatening to take justice out of the hands of the law and to administer it privately and wrongly. No one has the right to take justice into his own hands. The Jews are not responsible for the crimes of Bela Kun, simply because he was a Jew, any more than they may all be given distinction because of the courage and righteous patriotism of those Jews who were imprisoned with me. Are you as Catholics willing to be punished for the crimes of other Catholics? Will you condemn all Protestants because some Protestants are wicked men?

"Let everyone understand and tell it far and wide: Law has returned to Hungary and will punish the guilty who are taken; for those who are guilty and who have escaped, it is impossible to substitute the innocent. We did not get rid of criminals in order that we ourselves might commit new crimes. The blood of innocents cries to God, and will continue to do so, regardless of who sheds it."

That no pogrom took place in Zalaegerszeg, that the irresponsible passions of the mob were not let loose there, is in no little part due to the calm, wise leadership of Mindszenty during the early days of the liberation. Credit must also be given to Bishop Janos Mikes, Count Antal Sigray, the new government's Commissar, and Baron Antal Lehar, a Colonel and the brother of the famous composer, who promptly arrived at Szombathely with a newly established battalion of the National Army.

Mikes, who had escaped from the hands of the Reds a month before and had been hiding in the home of a relative, immediately sent a message to his diocese: "It is my wish that not one drop of blood be spilled in my diocese. Civilized man can judge his fellow man only in a court of law."

Bela Kun and his many guilty companions had escaped, but sometime later he and a number of the other Commissars of the Hungarian regime were executed in Russia as Trotzkyists. Thus once more was it shown that he who lives by the sword shall die by the sword—frequently, as the Communists have proved so often, by a sword held in the hand of one whom he has called brother and ally!

August 20th is St. Stephen's day which is the greatest feast day in Hungary. On St. Stephen's day, 1919, Bishop Mikes returned to Szombathely. A tremendous crowd made up of the people of Szombathely, its surroundings and the whole diocese, celebrated his return. The procession was led by Count Antal Sigray and Baron Lehar at the head of a battalion of soldiers. Mindszenty was also in the crowd, modest and quiet. In the evening the hostages of Szombathely and its surroundings, those who had

AFTER THE COMMUNE

been imprisoned by the Communists, had supper together. Mindszenty was very quiet and withdrawn. The others tried to make him talk, to rekindle in him the spark of vivacity which had been so apparent in prison.

"Was your Reverence afraid when they arrested you?" they asked.

"Yes, I was afraid," he said quietly.

"Were you very much afraid?"

"Very much afraid indeed."

"How much afraid were you?"

Mindszenty smiled at last.

"Well at the beginning of the war I saw a caricature. On one side of the picture stood a half-naked giant clad in a tiger's skin beside a tiny wooden gun. On the other side of the picture beside an enormous modern gun stood a young officer in a smart uniform. Both were plainly very nervous. The giant asked the officer, 'Lieutenant, are you afraid?'—'If you were as afraid as I am,' replied the Lieutenant, 'you would have run away long ago.'"

It was a typical Mindszenty story.

After the dinner, Bishop Mikes received the young priest in the Bishop's Castle.

"My congratulations, your Reverence," he said. "You were greatly appreciated by the Reds. They arrested you twenty days before they did your Bishop. Well, we appreciate you too."

This is how Mindszenty became administrator in Zalaegerszeg when he was not quite 28 years old. This is how he became parish-priest of Zalaegerszeg and rural dean of the district in 1921. In 1924 he received the honorary title of Abbe of Porno.

VI
"The Pope of Zala"

WHEN he became parish-priest of Zalaegerszeg Mindszenty began to build a new parish. New churches were erected, convents, homes and schools built. He demanded great sacrifices from the Catholics. Church taxes were, in some years, as high as state taxes. He himself lived in extreme frugality, with his mother keeping house for him. He was punctual to the minute in his schedule of living and demanded punctuality from everyone.

There is a characteristic story about him, illustrating both his love of punctuality, and his sense of justice. One morning a peasant came to the parish house and asked for a copy of his certificate of baptism.

"I shall have it ready this morning," Mindszenty told him. "You may come and fetch it before twelve o'clock."

It was after twelve when the peasant came and Mindszenty was sitting at table with his mother and his priests.

"Didn't I tell you to come before twelve o'clock?" he asked sternly.

"Excuse me your Reverence," the peasant faltered, "but I was looking around."

"What were you looking at?"

"At the buildings which your Reverence is erecting," the man explained.

"Then it's all right. If there's any fault, it is mine, for I am the one who is doing the building."

"THE POPE OF ZALA"

He soon was recognized by his curates and the teachers of religion in the schools as a severe disciplinarian. He demanded the strictest fulfillment of their duties from them. In his parish the teachers of religion had to give thirty-two to thirty-six lessons a week. In other places they gave only twenty lessons.

If one of them complained that the work was too hard, he was ready with the stern reply:

"The priesthood is not play. It is duty. It is work. If a life of ease is what you wanted, you should have chosen another vocation."

It is told of him that one day he called one of his young chaplains into his office. Without preliminaries Mindszenty said, "Last night I saw you walking along the river bank with a young widow. In the first place I consider it improper for a young priest to be walking on a lonely road at night; in the second place I consider it incorrect for him to walk at night with a widow; in the third place, since you did these things you should ask for your transfer. Please do so."

His reputation for firmness was well known to the government. When the Finance Minister began to cut state appropriations for religious and social work, he hesitated when he came to Zala County. "Better leave that alone," he said. "The priest there is a tough fellow."

Hungary was at this time in the throes of trying to establish a stable government on the remnant of its former territory left to it by the Trianon Peace Treaty which had been dictated by the Big Four. Seventy-one percent of its land, and sixty-three percent of its people had been given to other states. Impoverished by war and revolution, shaken by political turmoil, the people were restless and in need of a new hope and a new vision. Predominantly they believed in the Monarchy—then represented by the exiled King Charles IV, who was living in Switzerland while the government was in the hands of the regent, Nicholas Horthy, who had been elected to power in March, 1921.

A large number of the people wanted a king, but as to who he should be, there was a strong difference of opinion. The Legitimists stood solidly for the return of Charles IV to the throne, the Anti-Habsburgs for the free election of a new dynasty.

When, after the King had made two futile attempts to regain his throne by returning personally to Hungary in 1921, he was taken to the Island of Madeira by the British, and there he died. Then the Legitimists transferred their allegiance to the young Archduke Otto, eldest son of the King.

Mindszenty was by conviction a Legitimist, and never concealed the fact. He believed in the restoration of the Monarchy, and the re-union of Austria and Hungary.

"Little countries are at the mercy of the Germans and the Russians," he would say, when asked for his opinion. "They cannot defend themselves against the aggressive propaganda of powerful bordering states. We, and the whole world, shall pay dearly for the Monarchy's division. The price will be war, which it would be possible to avoid through maintaining a unity in the Danubian valley to balance the power of the Russians and the Germans. The world is ruled with little wisdom."

In politics he first belonged to the Liberal-Christian party of Count Gyula Andrassy. When this was defeated he followed the Legitimist-Christian tendency of Miklos Griger. He had little sympathy with the Horthyists, who although they declared themselves in favor of the Habsburgs, in reality, wanted to postpone the whole question, evading it through procrastination, while keeping the power themselves.

By 1930 his opposition became so strong that he expressed it openly. On St. Nicholas' day, the name-day of the Regent Nicholas Horthy, Mindszenty did not celebrate the solemn mass. This was considered an offense by the local military command. They denounced the priest to the Ministry of Defense, who handed the denunciation over to the Ministry of Public Education. The Bishop of Szombathely, who was requested to give the Ministry an explanation, laid the request aside without reply and the matter was dropped. The next year Mindszenty again did not celebrate mass.

His power and influence became stronger and stronger. Gradually the Bishop entrusted him with more and more of the supervision of ecclesiastic life and the direction of social service for the whole territory of Zala County. Though a frail man, Mindszenty seemed indefatigable, his energy inexhaustible. He drove his priests hard in the fulfillment of their duties, but he drove himself harder. He appeared everywhere in person, supervising, guiding, encouraging and disciplining when necessary. Soon he became known as "The Pope of Zala."

There were 16,000 Catholics in Zalaegerszeg. It is almost literally true that Mindszenty became personally acquainted with every one of them, and with the habits and reputation of each. He knew which came to church and confession, and which did not, which fulfilled his civil, as well as religious duties, and which had lost the trust and respect of his neighbors. He knew the neighborhood quarrels and family feuds, the domestic strifes, the mother-in-law troubles of his parishioners, their petty sexual derelictions and illict love affairs, even who, among the girls and boys, were the notorious shirkers of their school duties.

This was in conformance with a basic principle which he impressed over and over again upon the priests under him: a priest is responsible for his congregation, a priest must constantly be aware of the detailed conduct of his flock.

Much of his intimate knowledge was locked tightly within his aloof silences, never to be mentioned even in reproof to those most intimately concerned. But often intimations of what he knew would come out in the form of subtle pressure, used to gain his ends of social service. A case in point is a story connected with his milk distribution.

He had six cows, and used but little milk for his own household. The bulk of it, and in addition some which he bought from others, went to the poor of his parish. Every day he gave away over a hundred and fifty quarts to the children of those who could not afford to buy it. The distribution, scheduled for eight in the morning, in time for the children's breakfast, took place at the schoolhouse under the direction of a young woman who, Mindszenty knew, was having an illicit (though so far unconfessed) love affair with a married man.

One morning he went to the school, some little time after eight, to see how the milk distribution was going.

"THE POPE OF ZALA" 55

The milk was there waiting, the place was thronged with children, also waiting, but the woman supposedly in charge was not there. Taking off his jacket and rolling up his sleeves, Mindszenty proceeded with the distribution himself.

At about nine o'clock the woman came along, horrified and deeply embarrassed to see the priest at her work. When he asked her where she had been, she said that she had been to church. "I go to mass at eight, your Reverence, and distribute the milk at nine."

"The children are hungry at eight," he said. "Beginning tomorrow you must go to mass at seven and distribute the milk at eight."

"But your Reverence," she protested, "I would have to be up at six in order to have my breakfast. It is too much!"

He raised the little finger of his right hand, shaking it at her gently in one of his characteristic gestures of admonition.

"It is better to be in bed early—in your own bed, Mary," he said, "and to be at mass early."

Mary knew what he meant. After that day the milk distribution began promptly at eight each morning.

He early came into conflict with an old custom and an old superstition. The people believed that Saturday was the most auspicious day for a wedding—the couple wedded on Saturday would be happily married. So weddings were invariably held on Saturday. But they also believed that it was definitely unlucky for the bride and groom to leave the wedding-supper table before the dawn of another day. And so, on the Sunday after a wedding there were many empty spaces in the church pews—for all the wedding guests were sleeping.

Mindszenty corrected this by forbidding Saturday weddings in Zalaegerszeg. The people grumbled, complained in vain to the Bishop, and then accepted the inevitable.

There were other old customs however which he defended against attack. When a group of religious busybodies came and pointed out to him that the practice of spilling new wine on the floor or ground was paganistic and blasphemous, Mindszenty said, "It is a very old, and a humble custom. You do not complain when the priests bless the wheat crop. That, too, is an old custom, born of love for the earth. Yet you do not call that irreligious. No more is the offering of wine. God does not object to this simple giving of thanks to the good earth."

He was most assiduous in his concern for the poor, and would go to great lengths to see that they were not hungry, increasing the number of social workers, giving them special instructions, visiting the most poverty stricken himself, sending food from his own kitchen so that often his mother was hard put to it to find anything for his own table. On Christmas Day he always made many personal visits—always to the needy—and while he was on his rounds his congregation would set up the Christmas tree in his room.

As to heat—his visitors in winter complained constantly about the frigid temperature of his house. "Until I know that every poor man has fuel," Mindszenty said, "the parish priest will not have heat."

One of his most constantly repeated sayings was, "Poverty must not be tolerated."

Every Wednesday he invited seventeen guests to dinner—seventeen of the poorest of his parish—always a different seventeen—and served them exactly what he himself ate on other days.

Elizabeth Ruby, a former social worker of Zalaegerszeg, writing in a Hungarian newspaper has told how one of his most ambitious projects was suggested to him by a half-eaten onion which apparently was the entire meal of a woman who had just borne a child.

He had a list made of all widows and orphans and knew when every poor woman in the city was going to be delivered of a child and always called on her, carrying a huge shopping bag filled with food. The kitchen of the parish house was constantly busy keeping the bag full.

One day two of his social workers, Sister Palma Tecsy and Sister Gisella Rossler, coming into a miserable suburban cottage to visit the mother of a newly born child found Mindszenty sitting at her bedside with his well-filled shopping bag on the floor. The baby was lying in bed with his mother. Six other small children of graduated sizes were standing against the wall looking like organ pipes.

"Come here, children," Mindszenty said softly. "I want to tell you a story."

Now the organ pipes became frightened lambs in a storm, shrinking fearfully into a corner. Mindszenty reached both hands into his shopping bag and brought out two fists full of cookies, holding them toward the children and smiling. The children looked at each other anxiously, questioningly, each seeking support from the others. Finally they came forward hesitantly and took the cookies. Mindszenty put an arm around the oldest, a ten year old girl.

"What did you have to eat today?" he asked.

"I had some milk."

"Do you get it from the milk distribution?"

"Yes, your Reverence, I go every morning for it."

"And bread?" he asked gently. "Did you have bread, too?"

"Yesterday we had some bread as well as milk," she said, her voice rising happily as though it were the most marvelous thing in the world that for one day, at least, there had been bread to eat.

Mindszenty's face darkened. He looked at the two social workers, who were standing by listening.

"Please, ladies," he urged them, "do what it is you came here to do. Do not let me interrupt you. I would like to see how you will handle this."

The two Sisters signed the midwife's journal and then gave the mother careful and detailed instructions as to what she could eat and what she must refrain from eating in order to keep her nursing child healthy. Mindszenty listened without comment until they had finished, then he bowed to them gravely.

"Excellent advice," he said sarcastically. "There is only one thing missing. You have not told her where she is to get the excellent food you have recommended. I ask you please, my dear ladies, to look at this."

He took from beneath him, where it had been lying on the chair on which he sat, a half-eaten raw onion.

"I'm afraid that I interrupted this good woman's meal when I came in," he said. "Do you know any way to change this into the food you have been talking about? This onion is an accusation against Zalaegerszeg—against the entire world. It is a murderer of babies and we are responsible for it. It's all very well to sign the midwife's journal and tell the mother what she ought to eat, but that's less than half the task. The rest is to see that she has the food that you have recommended."

He rose and placed his hands on the shoulders of the two Sisters.

"You are in the service of Christ?" he asked softly.

"Forever, your Reverence."

"Then here at the bedside of this woman and baby and before the eyes of these innocent children, with this half-eaten onion as an awful warning, we shall make a plan to serve Him better. But first let us feed them. Everything in my bag is for them. The hot soup is for the mother."

While the children greedily ate roast chicken and white bread and the mother gratefully drank her hot soup, Mindszenty explained his plan to the two Sisters. There were six social workers attached to the church. He instructed Sister Palma and Sister Gisella to call the others together that evening and in his name to send invitations to those in the parish who were financially able to help, whether they were Catholics, Protestants, or Jews. They were all to be asked to come to a meeting at the high school on the following Monday.

At the meeting the great hall was crowded with men and women from every walk of life. Mindszenty himself was on the platform to conduct the meeting and present his plan.

"In an average week," he began, "five children are born to the poor of Zalaegerszeg. It has long been our custom to call upon the mothers in order to supervise hygiene and give them instructions in care and feeding, but we must go further than that. We must take care not only of the mother and the newly born but see that the other children of the family are well-fed. I want each of you to agree to feed such a family for two weeks."

Fifty-six women responded. Mindszenty himself agreed to be responsible for five families. Thus began one of the most successful pieces of social work in Zalaegerszeg, from which it spread to many villages and cities throughout Hungary.

One of his great concerns was the internment camp at Zalaegerszeg. This had been set up by the Hungarian Government, after the fall of the Bela Kun regime, in order to confine some of those who had played minor roles in the Communist coup. None of the internees had committed civil crimes. Undoubtedly many were unjustly imprisoned under conditions which would be considered shameful in the light of modern penology. I found many occasions, as a member of the Hungarian Parliament, to object to conditions there. But my objections, made before the law-making body, were, on the whole, less effective than Mindszenty's vigorous action.

As soon as he became parish priest of Zalaegerszeg he insisted upon a permit which enabled him to visit the camp freely. One of his first acts, when he found that no religious services were held there, was to insist upon permission to hold such services, and, having received it, to

"THE POPE OF ZALA"

conduct them himself, comforting and encouraging the internees, and championing their rights constantly before the authorities, who protested in vain against his "pestering" them. When abuses were not corrected quickly enough by authority on a lower level, he brought his complaints to Parliament through Janos Esztergalyos, a social-democratic member.

And constantly he insisted that the men in the camp be brought to trial, that the guilty might be punished, and the innocent set free.

The people watched him. Stories of how he had fought against this hardship today and that one yesterday, of his fearlessness before government authority, of his never failing helpfulness to the poor and oppressed, were told everywhere. His wisdom and unswerving sense of justice became strong pillars on which everyone could lean. No public question was settled without his advice. He became a member of the Municipal and County Councils, the leading figure in the affairs of Zala County.

It would have been impossible for any man to champion the oppressed as Mindszenty did without coming into conflict with, and making enemies of, the oppressors. Mindszenty had his enemies—and not all of them were among the Communists and (later) the Nazis.

One of these was a retired Colonel, Count Batthani, who bore one of the oldest and most honored names in Hungarian history. A wealthy man and holder of large estates, Batthanyi was enraged by Mindszenty's constant demands for high church taxes—demands which the priest supported fearlessly in public addresses, and in writing—

particularly in his regular articles in the local newspaper, *Zalavarmegye* (*County of Zala*).

Angrily the Count would answer his arguments, saying that Mindszenty was a hopeless dreamer, that he was trying to bring about a century of progress in a decade, that he was a dangerous revolutionary who was defeating his own aims by making the church so unpopular that it would lose all effectiveness as an agency for spiritual welfare. Never, he declared, had a priest laid such heavy financial burdens on his congregation. Who was Mindszenty, that he thought he could shatter all precedent single-handed?

Mindszenty never allowed one of Batthani's attacks to go unchallenged. He always counter-attacked, in words which flamed with fearless purpose.

"In what age has it not been demonstrated," he wrote, "that insuring the welfare of the people is the sole function of the nation? There is one way, and one way only, in which the healthy life of the state and of the church can be furthered: uplift the masses! Allow the people to sink in misery and ignorance and you destroy both church and state. School construction, church construction, convent building—all blaze the trail to a brighter future. Whoever does not understand this, whoever opposes it, belongs to the Dark Ages."

One day the Count could stand it no longer, and sent two seconds to Mindszenty, challenging him to a duel. The priest received them courteously, asked them to be seated, and then, laughing gently, began to make fun of them and the man who had sent them.

"Who's breaking precedents now?" he asked. "Many unusual things have happened to me, and I have heard

"THE POPE OF ZALA"

and read many unusual stories about priests—about how they have fought, with words, and with swords in the front line of battle. But never before have I heard of a priest being challenged to a duel. Well, there must be a first time for everything. It will make an amusing piece for the paper!"

Mindszenty had a goiter which troubled him. When he decided to have it removed he chose a famous Jewish surgeon named Dr. Erno Peto, connected with the public hospital at Szombathely. Before beginning to operate with a local anesthetic, Dr. Peto asked Mindszenty to talk constantly during the operation in order to keep the vocal cords moving and make them clearly discernible. With a flash of the same sort of humor as that which he had shown in prison, Mindszenty told this story:

"A keeper of bees had caught a swarm and was taking them to Vienna in a box which had a large crack in it. The compartment on the train in which he travelled had several women and a young college professor in it. The bee-keeper put the box of bees under the seat and sat down beside the college professor. After a time the professor suddenly jumped up and began to scream, 'Some sort of animals are crawling up my leg.'

"Realizing what had happened the bee-keeper took the situation in hand. Rising with dignity he bowed to the ladies and said, 'Ladies, will you please leave the compartment?' Then turning to the man he said, 'Professor, please take off your pants.'

"The professor, only too glad to be relieved of his difficulties, took off his trousers and the bee-keeper brushed out of them all of the bees that he could see. Then, to be on the safe side, he took the trousers to the window to shake them out. Just then another train came from the opposite direction, creating a great wind, which snatched the pants out of the bee-keeper's hand and whisked them away.

"The bee-keeper turned helplessly to face an angry professor, who demanded that he, the one who had brought the bees into the compartment and taken away an honest man's pants, should take off his own and hand them over. They argued so loudly that the conductor came in and tried to settle the dispute. Getting nowhere, he ordered them off the train at the next station and the bee-master, carrying his box of bees, left the professor standing helplessly and ashamed on the station platform in his drawers."

Here the surgeon interrupted Mindszenty.

"Stop it, your Reverence, please," he begged, "for I cannot operate for laughing. Please talk more seriously."

Mindszenty complied, talking of commonplace things, until the operation was finished. But as soon as the operation was over the surgeon and the staff of the operating room begged him to tell them what had happened to the bee-keeper and the professor, and in spite of the freshly dressed operative wound in his throat, Mindszenty finished the story.

"The station master nearly died of laughter when he heard what had happened. Finally he brought a pair of his own pants to the professor saying that the story had been worth their cost.

"You might think," Mindszenty went on, "that that is the end of the story, but it isn't. The following summer the

"THE POPE OF ZALA"

professor was at a teacher's conference in one of the towns of western Hungary and told the story to an amused audience there. When he got to the point at which the pants flew out of the bee-keeper's hand, one of the women suddenly screamed with laughter.

" 'Holy Lord,' she cried, 'so that's where those pants came from. I was on a train returning from Vienna on the day you tell about. Just as we were passing another train a pair of pants flew in the window of my compartment and dropped into my lap. I've still got them. I'll send them back to you.'

"And so the professor got his pants back at last, in spite of the bees," Mindszenty finished.

So far this is simply an amusing story which demonstrates the common humanity and sense of humor which dwelt within the stern "Pope of Zala" but unfortunately it has a tragic epilogue.

After the operation the story spread by word of mouth throughout western Hungary. It was one more episode which endeared the beloved Mindszenty to his people. Later, when the Nazi fifth column began to achieve strength in Hungary, Mindszenty rarely spoke at public meetings without having the story hurled at him by Nazi hecklers.

"What about the bees, your Reverence?" they would shout. "What about the abbe's Jewish doctor? Are the Christian doctors not good enough for him?"

A vitriolic campaign of calumny was started against Dr. Peto, and when the Nazis marched into Hungary in 1944 he was one of the first to be murdered by them.

VII
"This Man Fears Only God"

IT DID not take the Nazis long, once Hitler became Chancellor of Germany, to begin their activities in Hungary. Their principal medium was the Arrow-Cross Party organized in the early 1930's. Their emblem was a combination of the cross and the old Hungarian symbol of the arrow—two lines crossed, culminating at each end in an arrowhead. In western Hungary two of the principle leaders in the movement were the Eitner brothers of Zalaegerszeg. The Eitner boys, demobilized as first lieutenants after World War I, were sons of a wealthy landholder who was a close friend of Mindszenty's. They had told the priest about the new organization but had completely deceived him as to its true character. It had been formed, they said, to work for the revision of the Treaty of Trianon which had brought such disaster to Hungary, and for the re-establishment of Hungary's rightful position in world affairs.

It was not until 1935 that Mindszenty saw the similarity between their emblem and the swastika, or learned the true character and purpose of the Arrow-Cross movement. It was while he was travelling on a train with Bela Varga, a parish priest from the adjacent county of Somogy, and also vice-president of the Small Holders Party.[1]

[1] The Small Holders Party was a liberal democratic party made up chiefly of small landowners. Bela Varga, both within and without the party, was one of Nazism's most vigorous and efficient opponents.

"THIS MAN FEARS ONLY GOD"

Mindszenty, always willing to call attention to evils whenever he saw them, had been sharply criticizing the activities of some minor leaders of the Small Holders Party. Bela Varga listened for some time but finally lost patience.

"We are doing everything that we can in the Small Holders Party to protect the country against totalitarian infection from abroad," he cried. "We are fighting against Nazism without money and without power. You have both. Instead of criticizing us, why doesn't your Reverence sweep before your own door? I can tell you that there is plenty of filth there."

Mindszenty snorted.

"Filth in Zalaegerszeg?"

"Filth!" Bela Varga insisted. "Your Reverence is known as the mighty parish priest, the Pope of Zala, the strong man and the wise one. Why do you tolerate the paganism, the blood-myths, the racism and other imbecilities and the blasphemies and denials of Christ which are taking root in your county? Do you mean to tell me that you don't know what poisonous potions your friends, the Eitner brothers, are brewing?"

He paused and took from his despatch case several pamphlets issued by the Arrow-Cross Party of western Hungary, filled with the inflammatory doctrines of Nazism, its anti-Semitism, its denial of Christ the Jew, and its blasphemies against the Christian religion, and gave them to Mindszenty.

After having read them carefully with mounting wrath, Mindszenty called a general assembly of Zala County where he delivered his first hard-hitting attack against the

Nazis. From that day he (along with Bishop Vilmos Apor, later shot by the Russians) became the chief target of Nazi propaganda in western Hungary. Needless to say, by the same act he also won the support of all Hungarian Jews.

It was not long before he came into open conflict with the Eitner brothers, the sons of one of his oldest friends. A concert was given in the church at Zalaegerszeg in which orchestras and choirs from several surrounding towns took part. Large as the church was it was none too large for the crowds who came from far and wide. The places of honor in the front rows and the sanctuary were reserved for clergymen of all faiths from surrounding towns and villages and for the officials of the city and the county.

One of the pews so reserved was that which had been for years occupied by the Eitners.

The Eitner brothers arrived late at the concert. There was nothing unusual about this. They customarily arrived late for Mass, making a great show of swaggering down the aisle and occupying their prominent seat in the sanctuary. When they found that their pew had been reserved for others their faces flamed with anger. Immediately they hunted up the sacristan and demanded seats from him. After a long argument he got two chairs for them which he placed near a side altar. Immediately the two young men picked up their chairs and, carrying them three steps higher, placed them next to the main altar so close that the backs of the chairs touched the lace of the altar covers. There they sat arrogantly dressed in the bottle-green shirts which marked them as members of the Arrow-Cross and with the Arrow-Cross emblem prominently displayed on their sorrel-green ties.

Mindszenty, not wishing to disturb the concert, said nothing then, but afterwards he sent for them. Greeting them with flaming anger he threw a copy of one of the pamphlets Bela Varga had given him onto the table before them.

"You traitors," he cried. "You told me that your organization was interested only in revision of the Trianon Treaty, in the re-establishment of Hungary's dignity. Why didn't you give me this book when you told me about your organization? You are Jew-baiters, disturbers of order, attempting to destroy your country. You are sowing the wind and will harvest the whirlwind! And you dare to come into the Lord's house wearing that hate-inciting badge, taking it to the very altar, flaunting a Nazi demonstration in the face of the living God!

"Now as Nazis and Jew-baiters I ask you these questions. Who voted for your father as deputy? The Jews. Whose hand did he hold recently with tears of gratitude in his eyes? That of the Jewish surgeon who saved your mother's life."

The Eitner brothers, cowards in the face of his wrath, stood in silence, unable to meet his eyes as he continued.

"I forbid you to spread these hatred-inciting false doctrines. Further, I forbid you ever again to enter my house so long as you belong to this organization."

The two brothers left with white faces but immediately they called a meeting of their organization, reported what had happened and began to prepare a careful campaign of propaganda against Mindszenty.

This story came to me from Elizabeth Ruby, who at that time was a social worker in Zalaegerszeg, who attended the concert at which the Eitner brothers displayed their Nazi arrogance, and who was thoroughly familiar with what followed.

Miss Ruby has also given us the story of another encounter between the Eitner brothers and Mindszenty. The later story is also told by the Reverend Stephen Vidoczy of Catasauqua, Pennsylvania, who in 1935 was a student at the high school at Zalaegerszeg and often acted as altarboy when Mindszenty said mass.

On Holy Saturday, the day before Easter, there is a great and solemn Easter procession in Zalaegerszeg. The whole city is festively decorated; the entire population, regardless of religion, throngs the streets. Led by the dignitaries of the church, other organizations march with banners and floats in a long procession.

On Holy Saturday 1935, the procession started. At its head Mindszenty walked slowly under the baldachin holding the holy sacrament. His face, Miss Ruby reported, was a deathly white as if he were in a heavenly trance. His followers said that this was a common phenomena with him during such ceremonies, when he seemed to be completely enraptured.

Suddenly there was a whispering throughout the ranks of the procession. Directly ahead of the parade, standing a little to one side against the sidewalk, was Stephen Eitner at the head of a column of his Nazi followers, their Arrow-Cross necktie pins shining on their sorrel-green ties. They were obviously waiting to fall in with the procession as it passed. As Mindszenty came opposite them they raised their hands in a Nazi salute.

"THIS MAN FEARS ONLY GOD" 71

Mindszenty stopped suddenly, raising the monstrance high above his head as if to get it farther away from their desecrating presence. Behind him the procession stopped also. His eyes flamed with anger and his commanding voice rose high and clear against the whispering of the procession.

"Go away at once," he cried. "This is a feast of love. No organization based on hatred and lies is welcome here."

A slow, arrogant smile spread over Stephen Eitner's face, but neither he nor the men with him moved. Behind Mindszenty the procession surged, in an attempt to go forward, but the priest stood firm. Turning to the mayor who was nearby Mindszenty cried, "The procession will not move a step farther until these men have left." The mayor turned to a group of policemen, spoke a few words to them and the officers approached the Nazis. Still smiling arrogantly Eitner shrugged his shoulders and walked slowly away, taking his followers with him. A moment later the baldachin proceeded slowly and majestically forward and the procession continued.

This story was written by Miss Ruby for a New York Hungarian newspaper. She ended the story with this characterization of Mindszenty:

"This man fears only God."

VIII
A Bull Is Sold

FIRMLY convinced at last that paganism, in the form of Nazism, had invaded Zala County, Mindszenty, a thorough man, began to examine the country as though it were a battlefield, and to make plans for a long aggressive campaign. He had chosen in his youth to be a priest—and a soldier. Now he felt that he was being called to arms. He knew that his fight must extend beyond the borders of his parish, for his little realm of Zala was not an island; if Hungary were flooded, he and his flock would be swept away by the dark waters. The suppression of paganism was the job of the church.

Carefully he went through a roster of the Hungarian priesthood and made a list of priests, the ones of whose courage and fidelity to the ideals of Christianity he was most sure, and invited two from each county to an ecclesiastical meeting in Budapest. Here he addressed them, urging them to use every weapon at their disposal against the Nazis in their counties, and to propagandize constantly in order to counteract the increasing Nazi propaganda paid for by Hitler's gold.

"Where will the money come from?" they asked.

"Find it," he said, and told them that, in order to pay the expenses of the meeting to which he had invited them, he had sold the pride of his farm—his one bull!

(I remember a night when this story came back to me vividly. It was in the fall of 1947, in Paris. A mixed group

A BULL IS SOLD

of French and Hungarians were visiting my wife and me in our apartment on the Avenue de Lowendal. The apartment was lit only by a candle, for the electricity had been shut off, and it was cold, for there was no fuel. A deep silence lay over the street outside, for a great strike had stopped the buses and taxis. Paris seemed dead. Our guests had brought bad news. Trains had stopped running, they said. The gas and water were about to be shut off. Russian agents were blowing up railroad tracks and locomotives. Russian troops in Berlin were ready for a quick dash to Paris to install in power the Communist leaders Thorez and Casanova as soon as the strike had become general. Long lists of French and refugee opponents were ready, so that arrests could be made quickly. "If only we could fight it," one of the women cried. "If only we had money for propaganda!" Then I remembered and said, "Has anyone got a bull to sell?" I told them the story of Mindszenty and his little bull. With the telling, some of his courage seemed to enter that cold, dark room, and we all felt better. One little bull against the stream of Hitler gold!)

Meanwhile the Small Holders' Party, under the leadership of Tibor Eckhardt and Bela Varga (the Somogy priest who had first called Mindszenty's attention to the true nature of the Arrow-Cross Society) were becoming increasingly known as the most active of all anti-Nazi forces in Hungary. Tibor Eckhardt, the president, (constantly denounced by the Arrow-Cross as "a hireling of the Jews") became Nazi "Enemy number one."

The Small Holders held mass meetings constantly throughout Hungary, and Mindszenty, though not a member of the Party, and not in complete sympathy with all of their domestic policies, attended every meeting in Zala County, supporting and strengthening the anti-Nazi stand. When, in 1940, Eckhardt left Hungary for the United States, in order to serve the Hungarian cause in America, Bela Varga became the recognized leader in the fight, and Mindszenty stood beside him at every turn.

Varga now directed not only the Hungarian underground, but also that of Poland, operating from Budapest and Balaton-Boglar. Many a Polish pilot escaped through Hungary to England with false identification papers which he supplied. The secret Polish underground radio station was hidden at his parish in Boglar. It was he who sent out, on microfilm through Switzerland, the first authentic reports of what was happening at Auschwitz. It was he who stood up in Parliament to combat the laws against interracial marriages which the Parliament was enacting under pressure from Germany. Speaking as a priest he said: "You are acting against the laws of God and nature. The Catholic Church will never forbid Jewish-Christian marriages on racial grounds in spite of your laws." And in all of these activities he was supported and encouraged by Mindszenty.

Month by month the Nazi pressure became stronger, and the agitation of the Arrow-Cross and the Volksbund (another Hitlerite organization in Hungary) louder and louder. When the Volksbund instituted a campaign to induce Hungarians of German descent to discard their Hungarian names and take German names instead, Mindszenty, still known as Joseph Pehm, expressed his scorn for, and defiance of, their movement by dropping his German name

A BULL IS SOLD 75

and adopting the Hungarian name of his native village. It was at this time that he took the name Mindszenty.

One of Mindszenty's friends and admirers was Dr. Aurel Kern, Councillor of the Hungarian Ministry of Home Affairs. Throughout his political career, and even after he was forced to flee Hungary (in 1947) Kern's was among the strongest of the Hungarian anti-Nazi and anti-Communist voices. He belonged to the Anti-Nazi political group represented by Miklos Griger and George Szecheny to which Mindszenty also belonged.

When the Communists, trying to influence public opinion abroad (and especially in the United States) against Mindszenty before his trial, charged that he was anti-Semitic, Kern protested against the absurdity of the charge out of his intimate knowledge of the priest.

In a recent letter to me Kern wrote:

"Mindszenty's political philosophy was firmly based on the principles of western democracy. He utterly refused to admit the possibility of acceptance of any totalitarian doctrine. Particularly obnoxious to him were the racial theories of Nazism, which, he pointed out, over and over again, were completely irreconcilable with Christian morals. He called anti-Semitism 'the basest tool of Nazi propaganda—a tool which seeks to undermine the very foundations of Christian civilization.'

"I remember well how he expressed his feeling in connection with the anti-Semitic propaganda of Andras Csillery. 'Anti-Semitism,' he said, 'which proclaims hatred between men, violates the fundamental law of Christianity, which is to love. And if today we do not keep sacred and inviolable the Jew's personal freedom, his common and civic rights, tomorrow we may find that we have lost our own. The road of prejudice is a downhill road which ends in the mire of barbarism.'

"He had complete respect for the honest faith of a religious Jew, and only scorn for the man who was not faithful to his religion, whether Jew, Protestant, or Catholic. He believed that religion was the only sound basis for social morality, that it was impossible to be at the same time a poor churchman and a good citizen. To him the common law of civilization was embodied in the Ten Commandments, equally the basic ethical code of Judaism, Catholicism, and Protestantism.

"I remember a conversation which we held one night when I was his guest for supper at the parish house at Zalaegerszeg. We were talking about the Piarist fathers, whose school I had attended, and I was telling him about the excellent spirit which pervaded the school. I told him of the Jewish student whose rabbi complained that he did not attend synagogue regularly, and how the Catholic headmaster, Cornelius Szinger, called the boy in and said, 'Your rabbi tells me that you do not go regularly to the synagogue. If I receive another such complaint from him, I shall dismiss you from the school. There is no place here for a boy who is not faithful to his religion, regardless of what it may be.'

"Mindszenty nodded his head in approval. 'Wasn't Father Szinger completely right?' he said. 'It is a paltry man who does not keep to his religion.'

"On another occasion," Kern's letter continues, "in the

A BULL IS SOLD 77

summer of 1937, I spoke at a mass meeting at which Mindszenty was present. I was talking of the persecution of the church in Germany and of Cardinal Faulhaber's fight against Hitler. 'Who abandons his own religious principles,' I said, 'undermines his morals as well. This is true not only of individuals, but of communities as well, whether families, villages, counties, or the largest states. It is true also of every person, regardless of rank and position—whether his name is Adolf Hitler, Fuhrer and Chancellor of the German Reich, or Samuel Weiss, community schachter [1] of Lovasbereny.'

"At this point a Nazi heckler interrupted me, calling me to order 'for this grave offense against the head of the great German Reich.' There was considerable laughter in the audience as I replied, 'I fully accept the reprimand, and even consider it an honor, but I am somewhat confused. For I know the schachter of Lovasbereny very well, and respect him highly as an extremely honest man. So I cannot see wherein the offense lies.'

"Interrupting the laughter, Mindszenty spoke up. 'That's easy,' he said. 'It's an offense toward the schachter of Lovasbereny to speak of him in the same sentence with Adolf Hitler.'"

At the outbreak of World War II, Hungary, though a signatory of the Axis pact, announced its neutrality. Obviously the Nazis considered this a mere perfunctory gesture. When Hitler was completing his plans to march into Poland in 1939, Ribbentrop phoned Paul Teleki, Hun-

[1] A Jewish kosher butcher.

garian Prime Minister, to announce, as a matter of form, that a German army would march across Hungarian territory to enter Poland.

He was taken completely by surprise when Teleki answered, "We shall not permit it!"

"And if we march across without your permission?" Ribbentrop asked.

"We shall shoot," Teleki answered firmly.

Ribbentrop's answer was a mocking laugh over the phone just before he hung up the receiver, but the German march across Hungary was cancelled and we had no share in the tragedy of Poland.

In 1941, however, the situation was different. Again Germany announced that she intended to send an army across Hungary, this time to attack Yugoslavia, with whom Hungary had signed a pact of eternal friendship. Again Paul Teleki said no, but this time he knew that he could not enforce his prohibition. Unwilling to face the degradation which he felt the entrance of German troops would bring to him he shot himself on April 3rd. Laszlo de Bardossy immediately succeeded him as Prime Minister, gave Germany the permission for which it asked, and on April 9th the German army entered Hungary on its way to Yugoslavia.

At that time I was living in Budapest on the banks of the Danube opposite the Prime Minister's palace. My wife and I stood at the window with sorrow in our hearts watching the endless lines of German tanks, trucks, mobile artillery, army supply lorries and troop transports moving along the Danube carrying destruction. No Hungarians

A BULL IS SOLD 79

were on the streets to welcome them, no gaping crowds watched their passage. The people knew what their entrance signified and stayed indoors, mourning for Hungary's shame and fearful for the future.

And then began the period in which Yugoslavia's screams of terror crossed the Danube and the Drava. These were especially loud in Zala and the other counties along the frontier whose population is thickly intermarried with the Croatians. Jews whose brothers and sisters and other near-blood-relatives were being murdered in Croatia thronged Zalaegerszeg and implored Mindszenty to help them. He was powerful, they said. He and the Prime Minister, Bardossy, had gone to the same school at Szombathely. The Abbe must go to Budapest and intervene with the Prime Minister.

Mindszenty was a man of quick decision. He packed his luggage, went to Budapest and called on Bardossy. When he had told the Prime Minister in detail of the stories which had come to Zalaegerszeg and asked for help for the persecuted Jews across the Drava, Bardossy said coldly that he could not interfere in the affairs of the German army. When Mindszenty persisted he became impatient.

"Concern yourself," he said coldly, "with matters within your diocese and leave the foreign affairs of Hungary to the state."

"My request is supported not only by the Catholics of Zala but also by those of the entire country," Mindszenty said. "It is sad enough that I, an Abbe, must remind the Prime Minister of his duties, let alone that I should be reproached for it."

80   CARDINAL MINDSZENTY

"Your Reverence is forgetting himself."

"I am not forgetting myself," Mindszenty snapped. "I have seen Prime Ministers leave this palace dead as well as alive. I shall still be a respected Abbe long after the nation has put you out of office and condemned you."

The letter from Aurel Kern which I have quoted earlier goes on with the story.

"Mindszenty left the Prime Minister in a tense and bitter mood," Kern wrote. "That evening he was having dinner in a private dining room of the hotel Pannonia with several representatives of the Government party. I had also been invited as a high official of the Ministry of the Interior. A little before time for the dinner a well-known member of Parliament who belonged to the Government party phoned me to say that in view of Mindszenty's violent quarrel with the Prime Minister he and other members of Parliament questioned whether they ought to go to the dinner. I told them that I didn't know how the Government party members felt about it, but that I would be there.

"After the dinner a long discussion took place in which Colonel Timar, the Military Commander of Zalaegerszeg, took part. During the discussion Mindszenty drafted and signed an unusually sharply worded telegram to Hitler protesting against the slaughter of the Jews in Yugoslavia and demanding that Germany turn over to Hungary certain former Hungarian territories which Hungary would never have lost to Croatia if she had not held out to the end in World War I on Germany's side. The telegram was drafted in such exceedingly harsh terms that I suggested

A BULL IS SOLD

modifying it slightly. Mindszenty consented, and the telegram went off that night.

"After this I sent to Csaktornya (a village in Yugoslavia, formerly Hungarian territory, within and around which the slaughter of Jews was especially notorious) thirty reliable men to investigate the situation and take such measures as were possible. Further, Colonel Timar at Zalaegerszeg quietly and without any communication with Budapest marched to Csaktornya at the head of an infantry battalion (using as an excuse the fact that this was rightfully Hungarian territory), and occupied the territory until the end of World War II, restoring order.

"This is how Mindszenty saved Csaktornya and its neighborhood in 1941."

IX

Arrow-Cross and Swastika

BY THE middle of 1943 Hungary, ready to divorce herself from her Axis partners, began to send out peace feelers to the Allies. The most important result of these was increased pressure from Germany for further contributions to the already lost Nazi cause. When, in March, 1944, Horthy hesitated to grant unreasonable German demands, the Nazi army occupied Hungary, removed Nicholas Kallay (who had succeeded Bardossy as Premier in 1942) and put General Doeme Sztojay in his place. Immediately Gestapo rule was set up and the extermination of Hungarian Jews began. Before the Nazis were defeated hundreds of thousands were deported to concentration camps or slaughtered.

It was also during the month of March, 1944, a few days before the German invasion that Mindszenty was made a bishop (just as the people of his village had said, on the day of his new mass, that he would be) and moved to the episcopal palace in Veszprem. Immediately he began to make the increased influence of his new position felt in his fight against Nazism and the persecution of the Jews.

Shortly after he was appointed Bishop of Veszprem he visited Papa, the largest town of his diocese, to introduce himself to his congregation there and to make their acquaintance.

ARROW–CROSS AND SWASTIKA

After the official Bishop's Mass he held a reception at the parish priest's residence, where he received the various Catholic organizations of the city. Among the members of the women's delegations who came to pay their respect was Mrs. Dezso Sulyok, whose husband, formerly a member of Parliament, had been interned by the Nazis on account of his steadfast opposition to the Arrow-Cross. When the parish priest of the city introduced the ladies to the Bishop, Mindszenty stopped before Mrs. Sulyok, and said,

"Please Madame, stay here for a little. I would like to speak to you alone." [1]

When the rest of the women had gone, he came at once to the point:

"Your husband is interned, isn't he?"

"Yes, he is."

"Why?"

"For political reasons only. The present government knows that he is an enemy of the Nazis."

"I shall see that he is released," Mindszenty assured her.

A few days later Dezso Sulyok was called to the gate at the internment camp of Nagykanizsa to see a visitor, a young Franciscan friar who said that he had been sent by the Bishop of Veszprem. The purpose of his visit was to find out how Sulyok was feeling, whether he was well treated, whether he had sufficient food and what was the condition of the prisoners in general. What were their living quarters like? Were masses said regularly in the camp?

In answer to the last question Sulyok said that not a

[1] Literally translated, what Mindszenty said in Magyar to Mrs. Sulyok was: "I would like to speak to you between four eyes."

single mass had been celebrated since he had entered the camp.

Acting on this information, Mindszenty made an official demand of the police that they allow mass to be said regularly. The police acceded to this, but it is characteristic of the methods of concentration camps that, after one mass, the program of the prisoners was so arranged as to make it impossible for them to attend religious services.

The story of Sulyok's release was told to me by himself.

"On the afternoon of June 1st the commander of the camp summoned me," he said, "telling me that Bishop Mindszenty had come to Nagykanizsa and wished to visit me in the camp. The commander had refused to give his consent to this, not wanting the Bishop to come into the camp, but had arranged to have me taken by a policeman to an interview with Mindszenty at the police headquarters of Nagykanizsa.

"I met Mindszenty for the first time here in the room of the police chief, Joseph Buky, who had authority to free internees. I was brought as a prisoner before him and the police chief neglected to offer me a seat. The Bishop observed this and remarked:

"'I believe you will have no objections if Mr. Sulyok takes a seat?'

"'Oh no, certainly not,' replied the police chief, embarrassed.

"I sat down. The Bishop first told me that he had spoken with my wife and brought much love from her. Then he turned to Buky.

"'I would like to talk to Mr. Sulyok alone. May I ask you, sir, please to leave us?' he said.

"The police chief received this demand with a startled and embarrassed smile. He was not used to being thrown out of his own office. But then he got up and, with some reluctance, went out. When we were left to ourselves Mindszenty asked me before everything else to tell him honestly if there were any reason, other than the obvious one, for my internment. Had I broken any law?

"I assured him that I had done nothing illegal, and that the only reason for my detainment was that my political ideas did not agree with those of the government.

" 'Then I shall have you set free,' declared Mindszenty in a tone of complete assurance. 'You are not the only one who does not agree with the policy of the government. I myself do not agree with it. Neither does the great majority of the Hungarian people.'

"He called in Buky and demanded my release. The police chief looked shocked and incredulous. 'It is impossible, your Reverence', he declared.

" 'Then arrest me also, and I shall stay with him,' Mindszenty said firmly. 'If he deserves arrest because he disapproves of the politics of your government, then I do also, for I fully identify myself with the political ideas of Mr. Sulyok and condemn the present government as he does.'

" 'But I have no right to arrest your Reverence,' Buky protested, 'and it would give me the greatest pain to do so. I am also a good Catholic, and went to the same high school at Szombathely as did your Reverence.'

" 'It seems that your education has done you little good,' Mindszenty retorted. 'If it had, you would not serve the present regime. I demand that you release Mr. Sulyok at once.'

"'I cannot do it. It wasn't I who ordered his arrest, but the Minister of Home Affairs.'

"'In that case please call up the Minister by telephone and ask him to order his release.'

"'I cannot do this either,' Buky whined. 'As a minor official I cannot take the initiative with my Minister on such a matter. Please, your Reverence, you call up the Minister from here and talk to him.'

Mindszenty snorted.

"I won't speak, even on the telephone, with a member of such a barefooted gang as that to which your Minister belongs. Call him at once, please.'

"Knowing that he was beaten, Buky reached for the phone. Before putting in the call, however, he asked that I leave the room. But Mindszenty was still in charge. Though he had insisted, when he wanted to talk to me, that the police chief leave the room, he refused to admit that Buky should have the same privacy in talking with the Minister of Home Affairs. 'This matter concerns Mr. Sulyok,' he said. 'He has a right to hear what you say.'

"Sighing with embarrassed resignation Buky called the Minister, who said that he had not ordered my arrest, and had no objection to my release.

"'Am I not right,' Mindszenty asked, as Buky placed the phone in its cradle, 'in saying that your government is a barefooted gang? They all deny their own acts when called to account for them. That is why I won't speak to them.'

"The police chief said that he would arrange for me to be released 'as soon as possible.' But the Bishop was not satisfied with this. He demanded that it be done at once.

ARROW—CROSS AND SWASTIKA 87

" 'I shall stay here until Mr. Sulyok can leave with me,' he said.

"Thoroughly defeated, Buky executed the necessary order and I was free."

Luckily on that Sunday morning when German troops invaded Budapest (March 19, 1944) Bela Varga was in Boglar. Immediately upon entering Budapest, the Germans overran the Polish office, where Varga spent most of his time, looking for him, for his name was high on the list of those whom they wished to eliminate. Failing to find him there, they massacred the whole staff.

Varga went by night to Mindszenty in Veszprem. They considered possible hiding places, and decided at once that the episcopal palace of Veszprem was too much before the eyes of the Gestapo. At first Mindszenty wanted to hide Varga in the forest of the Bakony Mountains, at Farkasgyepu, at the house of a forester of the episcopate. Finally they agreed that a better place was Homokkomarom, where the episcopate had a house out of the village, on the ground floor of which parish offices were located. The furniture was ostentatiously removed from the top floor to make it seemed unoccupied, and Varga moved in under cover of darkness. For seven months he stayed there, only occasionally venturing out at night. The parish priest brought him food and news of what was happening in the world.

From him he heard of the advance of the Russian troops to the very border of Hungary in August. He learned of Horthy's dismissal of the Nazi tool, Sztojay, and his setting up of of new government under General Lakatos. He heard, with growing excitement of the entry of Russian troops into Hungary on October 7th, of Hungary's surrender on October 15th, of the German Army's repudiation of the surrender, their removal of Horthy, and their installation as Premier, Ferenc Szalasi, leader of the Arrow-Cross Party.

On November 1, 1944, the Jesuit Father Eugen Kerkai, a former pupil and a confidant of Mindszenty, appeared at Varga's hiding place.

"The Bishop has sent me with a message," he said. "He requests your Reverence to go immediately to Budapest to re-establish all your underground connections, in order to save the Jews of the city."

Bela Varga, who had grown as thin as a skeleton, made excuses.

"Tell his Eminence that I am unable to do so. Ten years of fighting have tired me. Seven months in hiding have exhausted me. I do not feel strong enough to fulfill this task. His Eminence must send some other priest. I'll supply him with instructions and tell him how to establish connections with all the underground forces."

"The Bishop believes that only you are capable of fulfilling this task. Jews and Christians equally trust your Reverence."

"The Lord is my witness, I do not feel fit. I do not want to shirk from this duty, but I am weak."

Kerkai left, but after four days he reappeared.

"I bring the Bishop's order," he said. "His Reverence does not request his friend, he orders the priest of his diocese! Your Reverence will leave Homokkomarom tonight. The

ARROW–CROSS AND SWASTIKA 89

Bishop's car will wait for you in Nagykanizsa. I have brought false papers of identification for you. You will come along with me to Veszprem, where you will receive your orders at the Bishop's place. On this same night you will go to Budapest."

Having both changed from ecclesiastical clothing to that of ordinary citizens, Varga and Kerkai left the lonely dwelling in Homokkomarom and drove by horse and carriage to Nagykanizsa where, in the courtyard of the parish, Mindszenty's car was waiting for them.

They arrived by night. Mindszenty was expecting them. His first word was a warning.

"Take care. All my movements are being watched. It seems I will be next now. Your Reverence cannot linger here. The car will take you to Budapest where you are expected. You will visit every cloister, every religious house, all parishes and churches. All religious institutions must throw open their doors to the Jews. They all must get false Christian papers. I know, your Reverence! Those who hide Jews are sentenced to death. But we must fulfill our duties."

"Does your Reverence believe that I have not fulfilled mine?"

"No one more thoroughly than you," Mindszenty assured him. "But a priest must fulfill his duty every day anew. Yesterday is not enough. Today is not enough. Tomorrow is not enough. Duty must be fulfilled unto death. If today we do not do our utmost to save the Jews at the risk of our lives, the ineradicable brand of shame will remain upon us. In Budapest your Reverence will execute commissions in my name and in the name of the Church. You have authority to give orders.

That same night Bela Varga left for Budapest in Mindszenty's car, accompanied by Eugen Kerkai. When their car reached the highway to Vienna on the outskirts of Budapest they began to meet groups of Jews being driven westward like herds of cattle by Gestapo men. Miserable old people, girls, women, children—all had small bundles on their backs and in their hands.

Kerkai woke Varga, who had been dozing.

"Your Reverence! Do you see the children's eyes?"

Marching between the lines of the Gestapo, some of the children held the hands of their mothers, others dragged themselves along alone, through the chill, foggy, November morning, their eyes staring in terror.

"Lord Eternal!" cried Varga and grasped Kerkai's hand. "Don't let us come too late! We are already too late for these."

From this moment, says Varga, he became his old self, animated by the vigor which had made the Nazis consider him their first enemy in Hungary. He set up his headquarters at a house of the Jesuit order. Jacob Reile, the prior (now teaching at the Jesuit College in Boston) became his first lieutenant.

"How many Jews will the cellar of the monastery hold?" Varga asked.

"A hundred and fifty."

"Where are the Jews who are in the greatest danger at the moment?"

"The Gestapo has headquarters at the corner of Kossuth

ARROW–CROSS AND SWASTIKA 91

Lajos Street and Semmelweiss Street. This section is full of Jews. These should be saved quickly for it will be too late for them. I have here in the house a German officer who has deserted and is in hiding. He will help us."

The next day, by a faked order signed by the German officer, the Jews were brought away from the Gestapo and installed in the basement of the monastery.

Suddenly the Jews seemed to have disappeared from the streets of Budapest, as if at a wave from the energetic, magical hand of Bela Varga. Parish houses, other monasteries, convents accepted them without question. They informed all those whom they could reach where an asylum waited for them. In cloisters or convents, in the vaults of churches, or in belfries, they found refuge.

One evening there was great consternation at the Jesuit monastery. A Jew named Halmos, known as a confirmed drunkard, who had been hiding there, had disappeared. What had become of him?

Reile, accompanied by a student, went in search and inquired at the nearest public house.

"Was there a rather Jewish-looking crazy fellow here?" he asked.

"The Nazis have just taken him," replied the landlord.

"Where did they take him?" Reile asked.

"How should I know? Probably to the nearest Arrow-Cross headquarters."

Father Reile told the student to run back with the news that Halmos had been caught, and instructions that everybody must be hidden away. For it was obvious that if Halmos had confessed, a Nazi slaughter would take place.

He himself knocked at the door of the Arrow-Cross building.

"Didn't they just bring in a lunatic?" he asked the guard.

"They just brought in some fellow."

"This man is the half-witted servant of the monastery," Reile said.

"He has a Jewish face."

"He belongs to the monastery," Reile insisted "We want him back."

There was a long argument, quarreling, abuses hurled back and forth. Finally Reile gave the guard a bribe and Halmos was brought out.

Now Father Reile was in a quandary. He did not know whether he dared take Halmos, who had risked the lives of the rest for a drink, back to those who might, with some justification, feel that he had betrayed them. But there was nowhere else to go.

As it turned out, his fears had been unwarranted. There is a natural bond of affection and capacity to forgive among the persecuted. When Father Reile and Halmos returned to the monastery the rest of the hidden ones embraced the wanderer with tears of relief and joy.

That night there was a phone call from one of Father Reile's associates in the underground. The Nazis had raided the Marianum convent where a hundred Jewish girls were hidden. Immediately Father Reile phoned Raoul Wallenberg, the special Swedish commissioner who, at the request of President Roosevelt, had been sent to Budapest supplied with money to help the persecuted Jews. Having told Wallenberg what had happened, Reile hurried to the

ARROW–CROSS AND SWASTIKA

Marianum, where he found the girls all lined up in the courtyard about to be marched away, to an unrevealed, but undoubtedly tragic destination.

Reile begged, implored, threatened, to no avail.

"The priests have debased themselves by becoming the servants of the Jews," said the commander of the Nazis.

"The priests have remained the servants of God," Reile replied.

Fortunately Wallenberg arrived while they were arguing. He showed the Nazi officer his mandate from the King of Sweden, and told him that the girls were under the protection of the Swedish Crown. By sheer energy and persuasion he won his point. The girls were saved.

Later, when the Russians came to Hungary they took Wallenberg away as an American spy. He has not been heard of since. But in Budapest there is now a street named after him, and every Budapest Jew thinks of him still with almost reverential gratitude.

One evening in the middle of November, 1944, Mindszenty appeared at the Jesuit monastery where he knew that he would find Bela Varga. Fearing he might not have another chance he had come to express his gratitude.

"Your Reverence, I thank you," he said to Varga. "I know that you will continue whether you hear from me again or not. Tomorrow I go back to Veszprem, where I shall probably be taken. The Nazi prefect's catchpoles are only waiting for the chance."

"Stay here, your Reverence," Varga pleaded. "Do not run into danger."

"Rome can find another Bishop if I die," Mindszenty answered, "but it will be hard to find followers if today we run away from danger. Believers are born through martyrdom."

He returned to Veszprem where, as he had known they would be, the "Nazi catchpoles" were waiting for him.

X
The Prisoner of Sopron-Kohida

D R. FERENC SCHIBERNA, a lawyer and a leader in the Arrow-Cross Party had been made prefect of Zala County when the Arrow-Cross seized power on Oct. 15, 1944. No one knew much about him, and no decent citizens cared to know him. He was a man who, in the littleness of his dwarfed soul, sought, through hatred and persecution, to debase everyone to his own level. He was an implacable enemy of the old order, and of the Jews. His first official act had been to imprison the former vice-prefect, solely because he was a representative of the former government.

The few Jews of Veszprem who had escaped deportation trembled. One of them, Mrs. Janos Peter, had been advised to seek protection with Mindszenty. We have her story of what happened. She was warmly welcomed by the Bishop, who hid her in the basement where she found twenty-five other Jews also in hiding. Every day Mindszenty himself brought food to them, apparently not wishing to entrust so important a mission even to members of his own staff.

But somehow the news must have leaked out, fanning to white-heat the rat-like rage of Schiberna, who, from the day he took office, had been waiting only until he felt strong enough to take the Bishop against the opposition which he knew he must expect from the people.

Meanwhile Veszprem was in a state of constant attack and defense. Every day Russian bombs dropped on it.

Every house was a lodging place for Nazi soldiers. Even the episcopal palace, with the exception of the Bishop's private apartment and a few rooms in the seminary into which the student priests had been crowded, had been requisitioned by the Nazis. And of course the cellar. No Nazi was allowed to enter that until after the Bishop had been removed.

On Nov. 27, 1944, Schiberna decided that the time had come to humiliate Mindszenty, who had refused to recognize him either as county prefect or leader of the Arrow-Cross, who had declined to receive him at the palace, and who had pointedly rejected the order to hold a thanksgiving service and sermon on the occasion of the Arrow-Cross Government taking power. With the Bishop out of the way he would be able also to take the Jews that were hiding in the cellar. Heading a delegation of officials and policemen he went to the palace and demanded more space for Nazi billets. Finding none he said that the theology students must vacate the seminary and be sent home.

Mindszenty was not present at the beginning of the interview, having turned the matter over to counsellor Robert Megyesi-Schwartz and the superintendant of the house, Szabolcs Szabadhegy. When these two told the Nazi delegation that the Bishop had expressly refused to give up more space Megyesi-Schwartz and Szabadhegy were promptly arrested.

At this Mindszenty himself appeared. "I demand that you release my two priests," he said, "and leave at once."

"Only with you," Schiberna retorted. "Your Reverence is also under arrest."

THE PRISONER OF SOPRON-KOHIDA 97

Mindszenty asked whether he had a warrant and Schiberna, having none, left hurriedly to get one. Somewhat cowed by the Bishop's attitude he now phoned to the commander of the gendarmery and asked for reinforcements. The commander refused to furnish them, saying that this was a job which would have to be done by the civil government, and Schiberna now ordered out a platoon of police.

During all of this the news spread throughout the city and when Schiberna returned to the Bishop's palace he found the streets crowded with people who had come out in spite of the Russian bombs which were falling on the city in order to protest against the arrest of their Bishop.

Within the palace the frail figure of the Bishop was surrounded by twenty-five of his priests. The sixteen policemen whom Schiberna had brought with him, all members of Mindszenty's diocese, hung their heads, unwilling to meet his eyes. There was a moment of silent tension and then Mindszenty turned and slowly left the room. The prefect with some of his policemen started to follow but the unarmed, black-clad priests silently closed ranks and barred the way.

In a few moments Mindszenty reappeared, this time clad in full Bishop's vestments and, followed by his priests, left the palace and walked down the steps.

Before the palace, a car stood waiting to drive him to police headquarters but Mindszenty refused to enter it saying that he would rather walk. They tried to force him into the car, fearing a demonstration on the streets, but at this the young priests again surrounded their Bishop and pushed the policemen out of the way. One of them ran to the car, released the brake and gave it a push so that it rolled away down the incline of the drive. Defeated, the policemen followed, rather than led, as Mindszenty started with his twenty-five priests to police headquarters on what immediately assumed more of the aspects of a triumphal procession than an arrest. All along the way people knelt on the sidewalks while Mindszenty, Bishop of Veszprem, walked to his prison, his head high and giving his benediction to the right and to the left. At the town hall the crowds filled the street from curb to curb, stopping the procession. Again Schiberna telephoned to the gendarmery asking them to come and disperse the crowd with tear gas but again the gendarmery refused. Meanwhile Mindszenty waited in dignified silence, and when he learned what had happened, he faced the crowd, spoke a few words to them quietly, and immediately the mass parted to allow the Bishop, his priests and the policemen to go through. At the entrance to the prison, he paused, turned, and saying, "This is my last benediction," blessed them all. Even the policemen who had theoretically arrested him, fell on their knees to receive his blessing.

With the Bishop safely lodged in jail Schiberna hurried back to the palace to take the Jews. Every nook and cranny of the cellar was searched, but not a person could be found. Mindszenty, as well as Schiberna, had his sources of information. Having learned that the Prefect would arrive on that day, the Bishop had quietly removed his guests to other refuges during the night. The story was told by Mrs. Janos Peter in Vienna in January, 1949.

Two days later Nazi soldiers again appeared at the monastery, and all of the inhabitants of the palace were

THE PRISONER OF SOPRON-KOHIDA

ordered to the dining room just as dinner was being brought in.

"Which of you took part in the street demonstration the day before yesterday?" the commander of the Nazis asked. Every priest in the room raised his hand.

"You are all under arrest," the commander shouted. And they, too, were taken to the prison. As they were leaving the dining room, one of the priests snatched off the table a casserole filled with "friars' ears" [1] and tucked it under his robe, so that they would have at least this much to eat in prison. (Ever since then "friars' ears" has been served traditionally at the monastery on November 29th).

It was not until the following day, November 30th, that the official order for Mindszenty's arrest was issued:

I herewith order that Mr. Josef Mindszenty, born in Csehimindszent, resident of Veszprem, Var St. 12, be taken into police-custody because he refused to co-operate with the authorities who, on November 27, 1944, conducted an examination in connection with military billets, therewith assaulting the representatives of the authority. Furthermore he attempted to incite the population by organizing a demonstration with his companions and by this act he jeopardized the public order, the public safety and thereby the interest of the military operations. I request the Royal Prosecutor of Veszprem to keep the above-named person pending further orders in police-custody in the

---

[1] A favorite Hungarian dish, in form somewhat like ravioli but filled with plum jam and covered with sugar and chopped nuts or breadcrumbs.

prison-quarters designated for that purpose by the Interior Minister, in accordance with Par. s 11–17 of the Interior Minister's decree No. 760/1939. Appeal against this decree cannot be made.

The order was signed "Dr. Ferenc Schiberna, Prefect, Authorized to act in the capacity of Governmental Commissar of Military Operations."
But the accusation contained in the order was not enough for Schiberna. The charges made against Mindszenty by the Nazis in 1944 bear a shocking resemblance to those made by the Communists in 1949. He was charged with treason because of a letter from Tibor Eckhardt to Bela Varga (which Varga had sent to Mindszenty) in which Eckhardt urged Hungarians to hold out to the end in resistance to the Nazis. He was charged with an "offense" against the person of the head of the State and with the hoarding of merchandise. The latter charge was based on the finding of 1800 suits of underwear which had been stored in the basement of the Bishop's house. The economic office of the episcopate immediately certified that this clothing had been a contribution to the Bishop's charity relief organization for distribution at Christmas 1944, and produced letters from a number of firms and private persons which confirmed their statement. But the authorities refused to accept this evidence and Mindszenty was condemned to be kept in custody indefinitely.

But even in prison Mindszenty continued to carry out his role as a bishop. There had been imprisoned with him ten theology students who were ready to be ordained and

THE PRISONER OF SOPRON-KOHIDA

Mindszenty insisted upon proceeding with the ordination, celebrating mass at an improvised altar in one of the prison corridors.

Following this, he was removed to Sopron-Kohida, a convict prison in western Hungary. A few days later he found a note lying on his bed which told him that he would be set free at once if he would sign a declaration acknowledging his support of, and willingness to cooperate with, the Nazis. He refused, and remained in prison.

Later he was visited secretly by Peter Horvath, secretary of the Christian Association, and by my friend, Mr. Hajdu-Nemeth, one of the leaders of the Hungarian peasants, who offered to help him escape.

"If the Nazis are planning to deport me," he said, "I should like to try to escape. If they are not, I shall take my chances on being released in the ordinary course of events. In any case I prefer to stay in Hungary near my people."

XI
Hammer and Sickle

ON FEBRUARY 13, 1945, the Russians took Budapest. Hungary previously had formed a provisional government under Bela Miklos which signed an armistice with the Allies a week later and declared war on Germany. The Government, under interallied regulations, was made up of all Hungarian parties, but the key ministries, Interior, Agriculture, Communications, Commerce, Health, and Social Welfare, were headed by Communists. Mathew Rakosi, General Secretary of the Communist Party, of which he had been a member since the days of Bela Kun in 1919, became Deputy Prime Minister, and the center of Communist power in the Hungarian Government, beginning the skilled manipulations planned to make him a dictator, subject only to the Kremlin.

Released from prison in April, 1945, Mindszenty and his secretary started on foot to Veszprem. Their road passed through Papa, sixty miles away. When they reached this city, Mindszenty learned, to his surprise and delight, that the newly appointed mayor was Dezso Sulyok, for whose release from the concentration camp at Nagykanizsa he had been responsible.

In every village through which they had passed he had heard the same complaints against their "liberators."

"The Russians have driven away our cattle and horses," the people told them. "They have stolen our possessions and raped our women and girls."

At first Mindszenty, filled with gratitude to the Russian soldiers who had freed him, tried to disbelieve these stories, telling himself that perhaps these villages had had unusually bad luck. It was not surprising that the Russian Army had its share of soldiers who acted like barbarians when they were conquerors.

"Why don't you complain to the officer in charge?" he asked them.

"He would deliver his grandmother to the devil," they said. "The officers are the worst. It is for them that the private soldiers take the women."

Having heard the same story in every village, Mindszenty's heart was full of bitterness by the time he reached Papa. He went at once to Mayor Sulyok and asked for a horse and carriage.

"I have only an old farm cart and a very poor horse, your Reverence," Sulyok answered, "and my only harness is a shabby thing made of rope."

"That will do very well," Mindszenty said. "I should like to leave at once."

"But would you not like to pay your respects first to the Russian Lieutenant-Colonel who is commander of the town?" Sulyok asked.

"A Hungarian Bishop does not pay his respects to the commander of an occupation army," Mindszenty snorted. Already the walls in Hungary had ears, and this remark was added, in the Communists' black book, to the notes which referred to his opposition to the Bela Kun regime in 1919.

Driving to Veszprem behind the decrepit horse of Dezso Sulyok he found the same condition everywhere. It was as though the Tartar hordes against which western Hungary defended itself centuries ago, had come back, killing, looting and raping, as they had done then. Veszprem was like a large family in mourning.

But Mindszenty was loath to condemn the Miklos government. He knew that so long as the Russians were in control it was impossible for the Hungarian members of the government to act wisely. The task ahead was to get rid of the Russians. Bit by bit, as he watched the encroachment of the secret police on the rights of the people, as he saw the people's courts becoming instruments of terror in the service of a Communist dictatorship and as month after month passed without the release of innocent people from the internment camps, he saw how helpless the honest men in the government were.

In March 1945, the landed estates of Hungary were confiscated for redistribution to the people and an economic agreement was signed between Russia and Hungary which placed all business and industrial activities in the hands of a state monopoly, the ownership of which was shared by Russian and Hungarian capital.

Meanwhile the Russian propaganda mill was grinding twenty-four hours a day. In the two newspapers which Mindszenty received in Veszprem, he read, for instance, of a Russian soldier "with a face like that of Christ" who appeared mysteriously in the cellars of besieged towns distributing bread to the hungry, of how Russian soldiers attended Hungarian churches in throngs to take devout and humble part in religious devotions, and of the tremendous welcome which the Hungarian people gave to the land reform.

Mindszenty himself had long known that land reform was essential to the happiness and well-being of his country, but he steadfastly opposed its institution under Russian pressure. He felt that it should wait until a Parliament legally elected by the Hungarian people could instigate it carefully and carry it out in such a way that it would really benefit the country. He disapproved of the cutting up of the great estates according to the Russian plan into such tiny strips that no one could make a living on one of them. He watched with dismay while fine orchards and vineyards were divided up to face almost inevitable destruction. He also protested against seizing the land without compensating the owner with anything better than worthless promises on pieces of paper. It was nothing more than a trick, he decided, to bring about the working out of an undisclosed plan.

His suspicions were confirmed by Bela Varga who had just had a talk with Eugen Varga (no relative), Stalin's economic advisor on Hungary. Eugen Varga, a Hungarian who had supported the Bela Kun Regime, had fled to Russia after the fall of the Kun Regime and there had become a Russian citizen. Now he had come back for the sole purpose of setting up the land reform. One evening Bela Varga invited him to a tavern and after Eugen Varga had drunk several glasses of wine he began talking of land reform, saying that he had always hoped that some day the Hungarian peasant could own his own land.

"Well, it's been done now," said Eugen Varga.

"It has been done indeed," Bela Varga said. "But how? I'm afraid the peasants cannot make a living on their tiny strips of land. It seems to me especially unfortunate that the great orchards which have produced famous Hungarian fruit for exportation should be split up. The peasants working individually will not be able to care for them properly and they will decay. Also many of the trees will be destroyed by peasants who want to clear the land for crops."

"Of course they will," Eugen Varga said, smiling cynically. "Of course the peasant will not make a living on his tiny strip of land. We know this. It is all according to plan."

"Then what?" Bela Varga asked.

"It's all very simple," Eugen Varga explained. "The country will not be able to export. The cities will struggle with famine. Even the peasants will not have enough to eat. Then they will offer gladly to give their land back to us in exchange for some sort of security and we shall set up collective farms. As to the former owners of the land, we are not concerned with them. They are a class rightly condemned to perish."

"Then it is exactly as I suspected," Mindszenty exclaimed. "They give the peasant land in order eventually to make him a landless beggar and a slave, and put him completely in their power."

"That is their plan," Bela Varga said grimly.

It was on this understanding of the real significance of the Russian land reform plan that Mindszenty's opposition to the method was based. Later one of the charges against him was that he had joined the landed proprietors in their opposition to the distribution of land to peasants; actually it was precisely because Mindszenty knew that the plan as it was being carried out would rob the peasants of their land that he opposed the Communist procedure. It is perhaps significant that when five hundred acres of the land of the episcopate of Veszprem was exempted from distribution and given to Mindszenty as a reward for his opposition to the Nazis, he promptly placed it at the disposal of the episcopate.

XII
The Symbolism of a Blood-Red Hat

IT WAS not long after the Communist dominated Government took control of Hungary that disorder, violence, and bloodshed began to spread throughout the country. In the spring of 1945, fifty people were slaughtered without trial or official proceedings of any kind in Gyomro, a village near Budapest. I first heard of the event from a Hungarian diplomat (whom I shall not name here) who was in Budapest when it happened.

It was during the summer of 1946. I was having dinner in Paris with three American friends at the Restaurant Tokay, a small dining room near the Palais Royal, famous for its Hungarian food and its gypsy band. A gentleman who was unknown to me left his table and, coming to ours, introduced himself as a Hungarian diplomat. He asked for a private interview with me, and I invited him to come to our apartment on the Avenue de Lowendal.

When I greeted him there the next day I took him to a room where we could be alone, and closed the door. Still he hesitated, looking around him at the walls.

"You may speak freely," I told him.

But he did not begin at once. Again he looked fearfully around at the walls.

"I have lost the habit of speaking freely," he said sadly. "At home—"

THE SYMBOLISM OF A BLOOD-RED HAT 109

"I know," I told him. "But here you need have no fear. The walls have no ears. There are no microphones."

Then he told me about Gyomro.

One evening, he said, members of the local Soviet rounded up the victims, some of them people who had made critical remarks, or who had opposed other governmental acts of ruthless violence, or who were simply disliked by members of the Soviet—the Catholic priest, the minister of the Reformed Church, some railway workmen, a number of unimportant unknowns. They took them to a wood on the edge of the village, shot them down, and buried them in a huge, shallow, common grave.

The secret police made a perfunctory investigation and reported that the people had all been arrested for offenses against the State and had been shot while trying to escape, but the relatives of the victims would not allow the matter to be hushed up so easily. Working through local members of the Small Holders Party, they sent a demand to Zoltan Pfeiffer, Under-Secretary of State and Deputy Minister of Justice, calling upon him to investigate the outrage, and apprehend and punish those who had perpetrated it. Pfeiffer waited until a day when Riesz, the Minister of Justice, was absent, sent the State prosecutor to Gyomro to investigate the affair and, undeterred by the threats that there were more bullets waiting in Gyomro, ordered the deputy police chief, Kalman Zsarnay, to go to the village, arrest the men and bring them back to Budapest in police trucks.

Seventeen men were brought back to Budapest and all confessed to having taken part in the slaughter. The next day Zoltan Pfeiffer was ordered to appear before Rakosi, who demanded that the seventeen men, all members of the Communist Party, be released, in spite of Pfeiffer's protest that they were confessed murderers. When Pfeiffer offered his resignation, but refused to order the release of the men, the matter was taken out of his hands. The next day Riesz came back, ordered the criminals brought to his office and without explanation set them free.

But there was still some open resistance left in Hungary. Vince Nagy of the Small Holders Party, a former Minister of Home Affairs, and at this time a member of Parliament, made a forceful though futile speech in Parliament in protest. A few days later, Mindszenty sent for Nagy.

"I wanted to shake hands with you," he said. "Order cannot be built on murder. The law must be valid for everyone. Every unpunished crime breeds new crimes."

It was some time later that I learned, while talking with Zoltan Pfeiffer in New York, the details of the unpunished pogroms at Kunmadaras, Hajduszoboszlo and Miskolc. In each case the circumstances were depressingly the same. Jews were killed in cold blood by Communists (some of whom were former Nazis who had gone over to the newly powerful barbarians), the criminals were arrested, the cases were taken out of the hands of the courts by Rakosi, and the prisoners freed.

During the conduct of these cases Mindszenty was frequently in touch with Pfeiffer, upholding him in his effort to obtain strictly legal procedure.

When Cardinal Prince Primate Justinian Seredy died in 1945, the Hungarian government sent to the Vatican the names of three priests, Marton Aron, Laszlo Banas, and

THE SYMBOLISM OF A BLOOD-RED HAT

Chrisostom Kelemen, the chief abbot of Pannonhalma, any one of whom, they said, would be acceptable to them as a successor to Seredy. But the Vatican had decided that the new Cardinal must be one who had strongly opposed the Nazis. Had William Apor, Bishop of Gyor, still been alive, there would have been a logical question whether to appoint him or Mindszenty. But Apor had been shot dead, in the early days of the Russian occupation, while he was defending a group of women against the violence of Russian soldiers, on a street of Gyor, and so there remained only Mindszenty. On a circuit of confirmation in October 1945, the news reached Mindszenty that he had been appointed as Archbishop of Esztergom, Prince Primate of Hungary. At the time he was in the great church at Papa, to confirm eight hundred children.

He pointed to the altar piece which represented the stoning of St. Stephen.

"May the time never come," he said solemnly, "when Hungarian Catholics stone anyone. Let them work with cordial love for everyone regardless of his beliefs. We are in a period of storms and disturbances, but the Hungarian Church has outlasted the storms of thousands of years. She does not creep into hiding when she sees danger approaching. She stands beside the Hungarian people defending their rights and unafraid of any power which threatens her. She is under the protective wing of God. She demands that every Hungarian Catholic fulfill his civil, as well as his religious, duties."

Later, when it came time for the new Cardinal-designate to go to Rome for the official ceremony, Rakosi hesitated. For a week the passport was delayed but finally it was

112   CARDINAL MINDSZENTY

issued (probably in the hope that its bearer would stay in Rome). Then, and only because of the intervention of the American Military Mission, Mindszenty reached Rome in an American plane . . . and at last, on February 18, 1946, Mindszenty stood before the Pope who placed upon his head and that of each of thirty-one other prelates (including Archbishop Spellman of New York) the flat red Cardinal's hat. As he did so, Pope Pius recited an ancient formula:

"Receive . . . this red hat, the sign of the unequalled dignity of the Cardinalate, by which it is declared that thou shouldst show thyself intrepid even to death by the shedding of thy blood for the exaltation of the blessed faith. . . ."

Later, according to eye-witness accounts, he placed his hand on Mindszenty's arm, saying, "You may be the first whose red blood will stain the blood-red of the Cardinal's hat."

And now his real conflict with the Russians began. Protocol required that he make an official call as Cardinal on Marshal Voroshilov, at that time Stalin's representative in Hungary. For a long time Mindszenty hesitated, unwilling to intimate by his visit that he acknowledged Voroshilov's authority. Finally he decided that it would do more harm to ignore the custom than to follow it, and he went. For twenty-five minutes he was kept waiting and then was told that the Marshal had been called away on an urgent mission and would not be able to see the Cardinal on that day.

A week later Voroshilov's aide-de-camp visited Mindszenty and asked him to pay another call. But Mindszenty

THE SYMBOLISM OF A BLOOD-RED HAT 113

had made his gesture to convention, and would go no farther. He sent a message back to Voroshilov: "Say for me that the palace of the Marshal is no farther from the palace of the Prince Primate than is the palace of the Prince Primate from that of the Marshal."

After this affair, Tildy the President of the Republic and Stephen Balogh a parish priest, who was Under-secretary of State in the Prime Minister's department, visited Mindszenty. They asked him to call on Voroshilov and have a picture taken together with him, so that the rumors about the affair should be silenced, and also to demonstrate that friendly relations existed between the Church and the Russians.

"The Russians must show us first," answered the Cardinal, "that they are our liberators and not merely an army which has invaded the country and who behave like an army of invasion. Let them first prove this by deeds. Friendship can follow afterwards."

In order to understand the irreconcilable nature of the conflict between the representatives of Communism and Cardinal Mindszenty, it is necessary to know a little of the part which religion, and especially Catholicism, has long played in Hungarian life.

The first laws granting a measure of freedom of worship to the Catholic and Presbyterian Churches were passed in 1554. In 1848 equal freedom was granted to all Christian denominations, and in 1894 the Jewish religion was granted a status of freedom equal to that of the Christian Churches.

Recognition of the importance of religious doctrine in

the conduct of State affairs was indicated by the fact that the upper house of the Hungarian Parliament included representatives from the Roman Catholic, Presbyterian, Lutheran, Greek Catholic, Greek Orthodox, Unitarian, and Israelite faiths (which together made up ninety-nine percent of the population.)

The Jewish, Presbyterian, and Roman Catholic Churches were very wealthy. They were large landholders, and sixty-five percent of the schools were denominational institutions conducted by them. It was fully recognized that the standard of education maintained by them was higher than that in the public schools operated by the State. Thus the influence of the Church on the cultural, social, and political life of Hungary was very great indeed.

The Churches—and especially the Roman Catholic and Presbyterian Churches—were the repository of Hungarian traditions of freedom and unity. Differing, as they did, in details of religious creed, they yet presented a common front against any threat to the freedom of the people, and often, through this, rallied the nation to a moral recovery. Religious differences were forgotten in times of crisis; the Churches stood for freedom and righteousness against all challenges; Catholic, Jew and Protestant stood shoulder to shoulder in a common cause. Thus it was during the Nazi invasion when Catholic and Protestant leaders made a common denunciation of Nazi methods, and became ecclesiastical centers of resistance as well as refuges for the persecuted of whatever faith. So it was after the Nazis left and the Russians came in. So far as the Churches were concerned any attack against religion was an attack against

THE SYMBOLISM OF A BLOOD-RED HAT 115

individual freedom. Knowing this—having known it for centuries—the Hungarian people were fully in support of the Churches and accepted their leadership.

Not even in Russia had the Church been so serious a barrier to the full implementation of Communist rule as it was in Hungary. It was impossible for the Communists to curb the Churches immediately without at the same time completely abandoning hope of ever gaining popular support for their regime. So, instead of a direct attack, they moved obliquely, trying to maintain an air of at least religious neutrality, while undermining the power of the Churches in insidious ways.

The first step was to diminish Church incomes by appropriating, in the land reform, the large Church-owned estates, thus robbing the denominational schools and advanced ecclesiastical institutions of their support. At the same time they attempted to prove their religious liberality by leaving the assets of individual parishes untouched.

Other than this, there was no official attack on religious freedom until after the general elections of November 1945, though there were several cases of arrests and abuse of Church leaders perpetrated by local Communist groups without the approval of the Party leaders.

The Party leaders' attitude toward such persecution as that inflicted during this time upon Monsignor Kriston, Auxiliary Bishop of Eger, and two priests from the Archdiocese of Kalocsa, would have been that it was wrong in timing—not that it was wrong in principle. They knew that, with centuries of history and tradition, the influence of the Hungarian Church (which was antagonistic to

Communism) would have to be liquidated before they would ever gain the support of the Hungarian people.

In the Fall of 1945, just before the parliamentary elections, Zoltan Tildy, a Protestant minister, and president of the Small Holders Party, visited Mindszenty and asked him to issue a strongly worded pastoral letter, calling on the voters to go to the polls in full force and vote for true democracy.

"The Communists are working hard now to stimulate quarrels between denominations," Tildy said. "Now, as never before, all denominations must present a united front."

Agreeing heartily, Mindszenty issued the pastoral letter.

"It was tyranny that brought Europe into this dreadful war," he wrote. "It was tyranny that trampled on the most sacred human rights. It was tyranny that denied, even in the statements of official doctrine, that the individual has a right to develop his abilities, his talents, his tastes. We must not have the kind of 'democracy' that replaces one ruthless, power-hungry clique with another. We ask you, our brethren, to weigh these words before you cast your votes. Do not be frightened by the threats of the sons of evil. The less opposition it finds, the stronger will tyranny grow."

In the ensuing election only seventeen percent of Hungary's votes went to the Communists. In Zala County, where Bela Varga headed the Small Holders Ticket, and Rakosi the Communist, eleven Small Holders candidates and only one Communist were elected. A coalition government was formed with Zoltan Tildy as Prime Minister. On

THE SYMBOLISM OF A BLOOD-RED HAT   117

February 1, 1946, Hungary was declared a Republic, with Tildy as its first President. But regardless of the form or personnel of the Government, the real rulers remained the same, the Communist Party and the Red Army, who ceaselessly undermined the efforts of the honest Hungarians who had been elected to office, and who were working against overwhelming odds to establish good government.

Meanwhile the attack against the Churches continued.

Before the war there had been sixteen Catholic newspapers in Hungary. Now, by refusing to renew licenses, these were reduced to three. All sermons delivered over the radio were subjected to censorship. Distributions by religious charities were hampered by regulations requiring that food shipments from abroad be turned over to the Communist Minister of Health and Social Welfare.

It was just at this time that the influence and renown of Mindszenty, already the Communists' "Enemy Number One," was greatly enlarged by his elevation to the Cardinalate. Further, he chose to mark the importance of his new position of national leadership by even more forthright attacks on Communist policy than he had uttered before. It was inevitable, under the circumstances, that the battle lines should be clearly and sharply drawn between them. Nor did the Cardinal once waver in his attack.

At Christmas 1945, in a violent address over the radio, he said that the most horrible event of the year had been the violent behavior of the Russian army. In a previous address, at a service in the St. Stephen Basilica at Budapest, he had given statistics revealing the number of Hungarian women and girls who had been infected with venereal diseases by Russian troops.

One of his most telling speeches was given in January 1946, on the anniversary of the canonization of St. Margaret of holy memory to the Hungarian people and connected by tradition with resistance to the Tartar invasion in the thirteenth century.

"Dear Brethren!" he said. "On this day when hundreds of thousands remember with consolation our Margaret, the pearl of our country and of our past, we have assembled in the Church to whom she belongs. My imagination flies to the year 1241, the mournful year of storm and horrors, of sins and repentance. I see the Tartars swarming towards the Carpathian passes, amidst showers of arrows, lances, stones and fire. Half of the Hungarian army is gone, including some of the first men of the Church, who stood their ground—the Archbishop of Esztergom and of Kalocsa, three other bishops, abbes, provosts, canons, and Knights Templar.

"The country fell into the hands of the Tartars. The swamp, the fire and the sword did their obscene work. Old people, men, children, women, girls, fell like sacrificial lambs. People who before had expressed no interest in churches and cloisters now turned to them for security against the Tartars, who were everywhere, piling the dead bodies of Hungarians along the highways and lanes.

"After one bitter year, when the powerful Khan died, the Tartars sounded retreat and withdrew to the last man. A decade and a half later their great power began to decline, and today it is only a horrible chapter in history.

"So it must always be, for sin will never exercise perpetual power over any nation. History teaches us that everything on this earth is ephemeral whether it is the

THE SYMBOLISM OF A BLOOD-RED HAT 119

work of Ghengis Khan, or of Napoleon, or of Hitler. God sends the world scourges, and agony to try its soul, but relief is always waiting ahead, for the hand of the Lord is on history.

"Do not expect me to draw a parallel between that time and this. It would be easy and I would not hesitate, if it seemed useful to do so. But it is enough to say: What has been written long ago has been written for us as a warning and a consolation that we may have hope and patience."

The whole nation sighed with relief!

"The Tartars went away," the people said. "The Russians will go too!"

This was final evidence for Voroshilov and his colleagues that Mindszenty could never be made to support their policies, that he would always be their enemy. After this speech, careful, well-planned propaganda against the Cardinal was started in Hungary and abroad.

Undaunted, Mindszenty continued the attack. Repeatedly he sent letters to the Government demanding that it cease abridging human rights. He called for the end of political persecution, insisted that the lot of political prisoners be alleviated, and protested against the expulsion of German minorities on racial grounds. Blasts of Communist anti-Mindszenty propaganda were the answers to his protests.

"He is a Nazi," the propaganda said, "a remnant of the Middle Ages, an enemy of the Hungarian people."

Early in 1946 the political police prepared plans to manufacture "conspiracies" in denominational schools which would justify action against them. Sometimes they misfired through carelessness. One such case was that of the Catholic high school in Baja. During 1946 the principal of that school read in a newspaper that the police of Baja has discovered in the school a plot to overthrow the Republic. The principal went at once to the local police, who read the account with genuine surprise, learning of the "plot" for the first time from the newspaper report. What had happened was that the "discovery" had been planned for this time, and the Budapest papers had been instructed in advance. But someone had neglected to tell the police at Baja to do the "discovering."

At about this same time plans for the abolition of the Catholic lay organizations were prepared by the Communists. Two events served as excuses. In the spring of that year a young man, member of such an organization in a small country town in northern Hungary, the son of a woman who had been raped by nine Russian soldiers, killed nine Russians in retaliation. A large group of the organization, and Father Salesius, a Franciscan monk, were arrested and disappeared behind the walls of a Communist jail, never to be heard of again. The charge was that they had "conspired against the Russian Army."

A little later Lieutenant General Sviridov, head of the Allied Control Commission, transmitted to the Hungarian Government a letter from the offices of the Russian occupation forces which accused Mindszenty and the Roman Catholic Church of fostering hatred against the Red Army. He called attention, as a case in point, to the recent "assassination" of several Russian soldiers in Budapest, which he said had been stimulated by Catholic agitation. Actually it was a well known fact that the soldiers had been killed by their own comrades in a drunken brawl, but the

THE SYMBOLISM OF A BLOOD-RED HAT

Hungarian Communists, without further investigation, promptly disbanded the Catholic lay organizations which long had been thorns in their sides.

By early 1946 it had become clear that Mindszenty was the Russians' "Enemy Number One" in Hungary. But so thoroughly did he have the support of the democratic forces of the country that political barriers to an open attack against him had to be removed as a first step. The Small Holders Party had to be strangled, partly through planting in it Communists who posed as men sympathetic to the Small Holders Party's policies. The Social Democratic Party had to be liquidated. The united Communist Party had to be firmly established and all members of national and local government brought to a strict line of Party obedience.

The press and radio both in Hungary and abroad were ready and powerful weapons in the fight against the Cardinal. Everywhere one read and heard that Mindszenty was a reactionary, an anti-Semite, a feudalist, an opponent of the land reform and in every way an enemy of the Hungarian people.

The following open letter, which was printed on July 13, 1946, in a Hungarian weekly published in New York, is typical of the sort of thing which appeared constantly.

"To Cardinal Mindszenty, Budapest.
"Dear younger brother: Though I believe that I am younger in years than you, I rashly call you brother, for how else shall I call you? Thank goodness I do not know you personally and am not even a correspondent of yours

but I get a big laugh out of your pastoral letters. If you wrote more of these I think that I might even collect them as a reflection of the state into which my unhappy country and our beautiful Hungarian language have fallen. Thus our Hungarian descendants might learn what kind of drivel a Hungarian Cardinal, kissed, appointed, and consecrated by the Pope used to scribble in 1946 in the guise of Christianity, which is supposedly founded on goodness, patience, understanding, philanthropy, and fraternity.

"You are stupid as a pumpkin, my dear fellow, you are ignorant, uneducated, and a fraudulent disgrace to the religion of Jesus Christ. You are simply a demagogic criminal whom the Lord would drive with whips, not only from the Cardinal's armchair but even from the tiniest village parish, an embezzler of the Catholic idea and the murderer of love, understanding and tolerance.

"I am not angry with you, heaven forbid! I pity you. If I knew that you were in need I would even send you food packages (but I am sure that you don't need anything for you live very well) and believe me or not, (but of course you won't believe me, for alas, you do not know what it means to believe), I would be most happy if you were converted, if you would become a Christian, if you would atone, and, rushing off to Rome, say to your boss, 'My dear Pius, I'm an idiot, but I shall try harder to become clever.'

"It is going to be harder and harder for you in Hungary to pretend that you have faith, for priests will come, real priests, simple and intelligent—at least for a time. After that if they again put Christ's gospel into a sack and start selling it as rotten meat on the black market, as you have done, if after a few hundred years new Cardinals like you

THE SYMBOLISM OF A BLOOD-RED HAT 123

come again to Hungary, then there will be another earthquake. This is the way of the world. Go to a cloister, Mindy."

During the summer and autumn of 1946 the Small Holders Party conducted a vigorous political offensive, trying to regain some of the ground which had been lost to the Communists, and the latter refrained from overt persecution of the Church in order to avoid embarrassment in Parliament, where they had their hands full with opposition based on former persecution and other matters. However, in December, 1946, the Communists were able to render the majority party helpless and to feel strong enough to continue with their program. Once more the Church was subjected to attack.

But when the movement for the nationalization of schools was launched in a proposal to abolish religious education and to introduce into the schools textbooks prepared and published by the State, thus indoctrinating the children with Marxist and anti-religious precepts, both Protestant and Catholic Churches opposed it so strongly that the Communists were forced to withdraw it temporarily. The Hungarian peace treaty had not yet been ratified; it was still necessary to take into account the state of public opinion, both at home and abroad. The nationalization of schools would have to wait a bit until the influence of the Churches could be whittled down still more.

With the resumption of the movement for State education the conflict between the Communists and Mindszenty reached new heights of bitterness. The more insistent the Communists became, the sharper grew Mindszenty's opposition. So he became the symbol of the whole nation's resistance, and the target for Communists' attacks everywhere.

Once, when riding through Budapest at the head of a group of priests, the priest-bearing cars were stoned by a group of Communist trouble makers. Mindszenty instantly stopped his own car, got out, and faced the mob. "If you want to stone the Church," he cried, "stone me. I am the Church." The mob scattered.

During the campaign the Communists brought every sort of pressure to bear on Mindszenty, and again and again frightened Catholics protested to the Government asking them not to take steps against the Cardinal. The campaign was carried on even through the schools themselves. Children were told to sign manifestos asking for the condemnation of their Cardinal. Those who were not willing to declare that he was a traitor and sign petitions for his removal were dismissed in great numbers from the schools.

Men known to have a deeply religious reputation were commanded to read aloud at village mass meetings prepared denunciations of the Cardinal. If they refused, they were arrested on trumped up charges.

Less important opposition was handled more summarily. There was, for instance, the case of Father Asztalos, priest of Pocspetri, a small village of eastern Hungary, who, in line with a resolution adopted by the village council, protested to the Government against the school nationalization bill.

Later, in June 1948, he held an afternoon service in his church, stayed to hear a few confessions, then left to visit

THE SYMBOLISM OF A BLOOD-RED HAT 125

friends. Many of his congregation stayed around the church to talk, and two policemen, pretending to believe that the meeting was in protest against the nationalization of schools, came to break it up. When a member of the congregation resisted one of the policemen, the latter's gun was discharged and the other policeman was killed. The man who resisted was promptly arrested and charged with murder, and Father Asztalos, also arrested, was charged with instigation to murder. After the usual "preparation" Father Asztalos was brought to trial.

Laszlo Varga, a former Hungarian attorney and member of the Hungarian Parliament of 1947, now a resident of Zurich, Switzerland, was present at the trial and in an affidavit has reported the following as a part of the examination:

JUDGE: You acknowledge that you were in Pocspetri when the murder was committed?

ASZTALOS: Yes, I was there.

JUDGE: When you left the church, were the people around the church?

ASZTALOS: Yes.

JUDGE: Do you admit that you did not ask the people to go home?

ASZTALOS: I did not ask them to go home.

JUDGE: Do you admit that you thus committed a fault?

ASZTALOS: Yes.

JUDGE: Do you admit that if you had not been in Pocspetri, this event would not have occurred?

ASZTALOS: Yes. I admit that.

JUDGE: Do you admit that you were thus the cause of the crime?

ASZTALOS: Yes.

The Reverend Asztalos was sentenced to death. The President of the Republic changed his death sentence to life imprisonment. Reports have since come from Hungary that he is dead, but there is no certainty.

This was a little case, the case of a priest whose name was no better known to the world than would be that of a village priest of Iowa or Nebraska.

Mindszenty knew that the case of Asztalos would stimulate no official protests from Washington and London, no mass meetings in New York and Paris. He knew that it would need the death of a better-known and more influential man than that to awaken the conscience of the world.

And he knew who that man would be.

XIII
The Tightening of the Net

MEANWHILE the Cardinal continued to voice his opposition to the Communist regime at every opportunity and to continue calmly about his duties as a Cardinal, living in the Prince Primate's palace in Budapest as simply as he had done as parish priest of Zalaegerszeg. Traditionally the Prince Primate's table is amply set with the most adequate of foods and wines, but Mindszenty's table was almost ascetically meagre, with no change from the rigorous fare which he had adopted as a simple village priest. On Mondays only one dish was served, during Lent he never ate breakfast, at noon he ate only soup and bread and in the evening only bread which he flavored with paprika. After lunch and dinner he usually smoked a cigar. When he got up in the morning it was his custom as it had been since his early priesthood to hum the tune of the "Veni Sancte" or the "Veni Creator," and before he went to bed he always sang the "Te Deum" in a low voice.

He forbade his parish priests to prepare big meals on the occasion of confirmation tours through the country. It is told that once, when his instructions had been disregarded, and an elaborate meal prepared, he rose from the table after having eaten his soup, saying, "Lunch is finished."

Jeno Szatmari, a Hungarian writer, has described a visit which he made to the Cardinal with an American journalist.

"The doorman," Szatmari wrote, "who opens the front door at the palace is a simple man. On his naked feet he wears sandals such as the Apostles wore, and silently leads us upstairs to the Cardinal's secretary. Along the walls of the staircase are pictures of the Popes. In the corridors there are reproductions of paintings by classic Catholic artists.

"While waiting for the Cardinal to receive us I notice on the wall in the large drawing room life sized portraits of King Francis Joseph and Queen Elizabeth, and on a marble-topped table two small photographs of ex-King Charles and his queen, Zita. Through the door to a nearby room I can see copies of paintings of Biblical subjects by the classic artists of the Renaissance.

"The Cardinal receives us in his small study as simply furnished as the room of a village clergyman. We speak in German.

"The American journalist mentions the fight between the Hungarian State and the Catholic Church. Mindszenty discusses it easily, calmly, freely, and mentions particularly the conflict over State education. He says that the Church is merely defending the rights of the parents to choose what kind of an education they wish to give their children and what sort of school they want them to attend. The Church does not wish a school monopoly, he says, but the State does. Whereas over sixty percent of the schools had formerly been in sectarian hands these had now all

THE TIGHTENING OF THE NET 129

been taken over by the State in order to indoctrinate the children with Communism.

" 'We want to keep our schools,' he says. 'We freely acknowledge the right of the State to build its schools but where there is a Catholic school it belongs to us.'

"He often stretches his hands over the table in the gesture of an orator and occasionally touches the red cap on his head as if to settle it more securely there. He is not nervous, he speaks calmly and slowly so that it is very easy to copy exactly what he is saying. Obviously, he has said this often before.

"My American colleague points out that the Reformed and Evangelical Churches have made an agreement with the State by which some schools are left to the Church. The Cardinal promptly replies that the Catholic Church is not interested in what other churches do and that it will not be satisfied with having a few high schools left to it but must also educate its children in the elementary school. The Church will not bargain, he says. She will not negotiate.

"He sees no possibility of an agreement."

Day by day and week by week through his public statements he swelled the Communists' entries in the record of his opposition to them, and increased the people's love and admiration for him. His journeys to the provinces became triumphal processions. Streets were decorated and arches raised everywhere to greet him. Festive, mounted escorts and guards on bicycles were sent to the outskirts of a village to meet him when he arrived. In Debrecen, the center of Calvinism, where only thirty percent of the population are Catholics, the Calvinist Prefect and the Social-Democrat Mayor went far outside the city to meet and welcome him. Then they led him to the city hall where the predominantly Protestant town council had assembled in his honor.

On such journeys he always went to great trouble to come into direct contact with as many people as possible. He went from group to group and questioned individuals about conditions in their neighborhood, as a priest might in his own diocese. He visited the hospitals and the prisons and inquired closely into the social work of the neighborhood.

Those who surrounded him were constantly urged under pressure to become Communist spies. The head of the post office in Esztergom became a spy of the Russians, so did Mindszenty's errand boy, one of his doormen, his typist and the superintendent of the Cardinal's palace in Buda. Whenever he stayed in Budapest it seemed to become necessary to tear up the sidewalk in front of his house and to repair the telephone wires. A factory near the Cardinal's palace was taken over by the Government who turned it into a dormitory for the eighty plain-clothesmen who were on watch in shifts twenty-four hours a day.

Month by month the Communists' strangle hold on the Government was tightening, though they still maintained a legal front. The situation is typified by the story of Jajos Dinnyes, who became Prime Minister in June, 1947, with Rakosi as Deputy Prime Minister.

Dinnyes, an old friend of mine, was a charming, amusing, cynical and good-natured man, who loved wine, women, dancing, money and gypsy music. Many of his

THE TIGHTENING OF THE NET 131

sayings during the time when he was in effect a dummy Prime Minister are now current among Hungarians. Shortly after he had been appointed Prime Minister, he met the newly appointed head of one of the big banks, a mediocre lawyer of Budapest. They shook hands and Dinnyes smiled. "Can you imagine to what depths the country has sunk," he said, "when I can be Prime Minister and you can be head of the state bank?"

When the Council of Ministers had to approve an order which the Russians had forced upon them and which was obviously against the interest of the country, Dinnyes said repeatedly in answer to every argument for and against it, "We shall be hanged, gentlemen. We shall be hanged."

When visitors came to see him he would point to his bare writing desk and his idle secretaries and smile. "You may see," he would say, "how active the Prime Minister is."

An American friend of mine who had also been a friend of Dinnyes for many years spent a night with him in Budapest and said that he wanted to speak to Rakosi.

"Well, you won't have to wait for him any longer than I have to," Dinnyes said smiling.

"You, the Prime Minister?" the American asked in surprise.

"I'm not the Prime Minister," Dinnyes answered scornfully. "I am dirt. If I want to speak to Rakosi I have to have my name put on a waiting list like anyone else. Oh, I have a lot of privileges. In the Prime Minister's palace I have the right to present my friends with lovely Hungarian cigaret lighters with my signature engraved on them. Would you like one as a souvenir from the Hungarian Prime Minister? I have the right to have my portrait painted at Government expense. In very minor affairs, I can intervene with local authorities, sometimes even with success. Very rarely I can even get a passport for one of my friends. That is what being Prime Minister of Hungary today amounts to."

At least once Mindszenty tried to obtain the cooperation of Dinnyes. On October 24, 1947, the Cardinal wrote the Prime Minister as follows:

"Mr. Prime Minister: The Hungarian episcopate has examined at its last meeting several grievances sent to them by their flock and which are signs of serious moral complaints caused by interior trouble. These grievances are as follows:

"1. People are forced to belong to the Communist Party although it does not agree with their conscience to ratify the program of this party and their religious convictions are opposed to it. These people cannot keep their jobs or find others unless they become members of the Party. Adherence to the Communist Party confers upon its members immunity towards all sanctions and punitive measures. These are well known facts; indeed a member of the governmental party mentioned them during a parliamentary session on October 9.

"Mr. Prime Minister, we hope that this deplorable situation which undermines the rights of freedom and democracy will be corrected after the elections. We consider it impossible that on the occasion of the centenary of 1848, at a time when we congratulate ourselves on the suppression of the privileges of the nobility, that again 'party privileges' shall be introduced destroying all equality.

THE TIGHTENING OF THE NET

"2. The second complaint concerns the system of secret control which the police wish to establish. Functionaries of this police choose certain persons, and even priests, and under pretext of unreal and false accusations, and by threats, try to induce them to spy on religious associations, at ecclesiastical institutions, and in schools. Later they must report all that is done and said in these places. One of these 'so-called spies' has been tortured because his report didn't correspond to what the police had expected. If one of them reported to others what he was ordered to do, he was threatened with a perjury trial. Such proceedings, incompatible with Hungarian character, remind us of the so-called Bach-period which followed the war for freedom in 1848-49. This is one of the darkest epochs of our history. The activity of these secret agents against the Church is totally uncalled for. In fact they seek in vain to find a conspiracy within the Church. On what grounds is such a suspicion based? Is it not apparent by now that it is our habit to say openly what we think? Our congresses and our publications, which unfortunately appear so rarely, prove this eloquently enough.

"Mr. Prime Minister, in the hope that these abuses arise only from the inopportune zeal of subordinates, we beg you to intervene that they may be suppressed and that every Hungarian can enjoy his peace without fear and trouble.

"Please accept, Mr. Prime Minister, the expression of my high consideration."

Dinnyes never answered this letter—indeed he would probably not have been permitted to do so even if he had wanted to.

Working behind the front of such figureheads as this, the Government continued its pressure against the Church. When the Church found it difficult to keep its schools open on its curbed income, the Government, in a gesture which it labelled "co-operation," offered to pay the teachers' salaries. Mindszenty rejected the offer, knowing that this plan would place Catholic education firmly under Communist control.

In January, 1948, Rakosi, announced that as a part of the Communist program for the coming year, "the liquidation of ecclesiastical reaction" would be affected.

When impatient Moscow ordered action on the school matter, and the Hungarian Parliament finally passed the nationalization bill in June, 1948, Mindszenty ordered all the bells of Hungarian Catholic churches to be rung in token of mourning.

When the Communists, wanting more than anything to be rid of him, told him that he would be allowed to leave the country in safety, he refused to leave. To a visitor at about this time, he said, "The wolf has more security in the forest than an honest Christian in the Hungarian Communist State. In four months I shall probably be waiting my turn in a hangman's cell. But I shall never change my policy or take back any of the things I have said against the Communist Government. God has ordained my fate and I give myself into his hands."

Meanwhile he exerted every effort to evade the ring of spies which had been drawn about him.

It was the custom for episcopal conferences to be held at the Cardinal's palace in Buda but during the last few months before his arrest Mindszenty would greet the

THE TIGHTENING OF THE NET 135

Bishops as they arrived and then take them by cars to a monastery—a different one each time—where the conferences would be held. Formerly he had sent an agenda to each of the Bishops who were to attend, but now he prepared one only to be announced when the conference was finally in session, and whereas minutes of the meeting had formerly been sent to all the Bishops, now only one copy was made and this was supposedly faithfully guarded at the Cardinal's palace. Nevertheless Rakosi was able later, in a conference with Bishop Laszlo Banas, to cite the resolutions adopted at some of these conferences, quoting exactly the page numbers of the supposedly secret minutes.

Month by month the press campaign against Mindszenty prepared the country for his arrest. The following series of quotations are especially interesting because they are taken from *Hirlap*, an old Budapest paper with traditions that go back many decades. Formerly a conservative paper, today, of course, every line in *Hirlap* is written as ordered by the regime, and every member of its staff is openly or secretly a member of the Communist Party. The final campaign leading up to Mindszenty's arrest began fairly mildly in *Hirlap* on November 6, 1948, in an article which said:

"All classes of Hungarian workers protest against Mindszenty's reactionary policies. The real motive of his reactionary activities has been recognized by the Hungarian women who, through various democratic organizations, have sent telegrams to the Prime Minister demanding that the government curb his agitation. Mindszenty wants to drive the poor people into another war, the telegrams say.

We protest in the name of all our fellow women and cry out to the world 'Enough war mongering; we do not want war. Forbid the meetings of the war monger Mindszenty.'"

On the 21st of November it reported the following from a speech delivered by Ernest Gero, Minister of Transportation, at the dedication of the rebuilt Tisza bridge:

"It would be a mistake if we saw only the successes we have achieved in the Hungarian popular democracy and overlooked the fact that there are some people who do not rejoice at our successes. These gentlemen must see that the people turn away from them while popular democracy takes constantly deeper root in our country. With their restricted reactionary politics they have come to a blind alley; they try to push their followers against the wall through which they cannot break but against which they may indeed break their heads. If this happens they have only themselves to blame. It is not hard to guess that I am speaking of the clerical reactionaries who make common cause with the foreign enemies of the Hungarian people and with their boss Cardinal Mindszenty.

"It is not our custom to threaten. We know that among Catholics there are millions who feel as we do and we also know that the Hungarian Popular Democracy is going to accomplish the task which it has set for itself. Now there has been added to that task the curbing of the Mindszenty reactionary policy which is calculated to drive us into a bloody war and destroy our country. The Hungarian Popular Democracy will accomplish this task just as it has carried out the land reform and the socialization of factory and banks, and crushed the Pfeiffer clique which was in the pay of foreign imperialists and Hungarian reactionaries.

"We shall not allow anyone to stop our constructive work or endanger the peace and security of the people. While our industrial workers are laboring, peasants and our intelligentsia work with all their force to eliminate the grave consequences of a war which ended only a few years ago, we shall not tolerate people who do not themselves work but conspire with the war mongers."

On November 24th under the heading "Three Hundred Church Leaders Protest Against Mindszenty" *Hirlap* reported a meeting of Catholic students of Szeged at which one said, "We Catholic students of Szeged realize that democracy fully secures freedom of religion. We wish to remain good Catholics but wish to put an end to the practice of delivering political addresses from the pulpit instead of God's word. Those who mislead youth as Mindszenty is doing should be forced to quit the leadership of the church."

Day after day the campaign continued. On November 26th *Hirlap* quoted the chief secretary of the Small Holders Party as demanding that the Cardinal change his attitude or take the consequences. On November 28th it reported a long address by Rakosi at a meeting of the Communist Party from which the following is quoted:

"This policy of tolerance which has treated leniently spies in priests' or cardinals' robes, traitors, foreign currency smugglers, Habsburg worshippers, fascists, and believers in the old reactionary order has now come to an end. It will also no longer be true that the law will punish only the little clerical criminals without touching the great ones.

"Our democracy is becoming stabilized everywhere. Our political and economic arrangements are completely approved by the people. Under these circumstances it is inconceivable that organized storm troopers of fascism and reaction such as those who are lined up behind Mindszenty should be tolerated. Their days of grace have run out.

"The fact that we have come to an agreement with the Protestant Church makes it clear to every person of good will that there is no question here of religious persecution but only of the righteous and inevitable defense of democracy. Only Mindszenty and his Catholic followers have refused to cooperate. Evolution now demands that we bring about order also in this sphere. If we cannot establish it by mutual agreement then, acting in accordance with the wishes of the people, we shall do so by the power of the State."

On December 1st, *Hirlap* again reported: "Students Protest Against Mindszenty's Inciting Politics." In this case it was the Sacred Heart Catholic Youth Organization which, according to *Hirlap*, had addressed a strongly worded letter to the Hungarian bishops calling upon them to remove from leadership of the Church those who dealt in incitement toward rebellion and war mongering. Other similar action by other youth groups was also reported on that day.

On December 2nd the paper reported that teachers and workers of Pecs had declared themselves against "Mind-

THE TIGHTENING OF THE NET

szentyism." On December 3rd it reported that students and members of the congregation of Eger had handed a protest against Mindszenty to the Archbishop. On December 8th, 10th and 11th it reported protests against Mindszenty from the Catholic priests of Trans-Danubia, from workers in Budapest, and from 2000 Budapest students. On the 13th another protest from a student delegation was reported.

Meanwhile Lajos Dinnyes had been forced to resign as Prime Minister and Istvan Dobi had been appointed in his place.

Dinnyes, in his devil-may-care way, had been a good fellow traveler, and an obedient servant. He had executed every order without a word. But sometimes, after doing so, he would make a cynical remark, and Communists have no sense of humor. They wanted a man who was secretly a Communist while presenting a traditional front.

Dobi was the ideal man for the purpose. Born a poor farmhand, he had become a prisoner of war in Russia during World War I. There he had joined the Communist Party, but returning after the war he had renounced his Party membership and joined the Small Holders. When the Russians took over Hungary in 1945, he applied to them for a job. They told him to remain in the Small Holders Party, to keep quiet about his Communist leanings, and to work against anti-Communist agitation. In three years they gave him many commissions which he fulfilled faithfully, while still seeming to be a good member of the Small Holders Party. Now, still ostensibly a Small Holder, he was put into the job for which he had been groomed. Unlike Dinnyes, he could be a front for Rakosi without making humorous, cynical remarks.

In his first speech in Parliament on December 14th, Dobi said:

"The first line of reaction in Hungary is assembled under the black banner of Mindszenty. The former government did everything in its power to establish harmonious relations between the State and various Churches. In the case of the Protestant Church their efforts were successful. They succeeded in establishing a lasting agreement with the Reformed and the Evangelical Churches which already have had happy results for both the State and the Churches. Only recently, at the Synod of the Evangelical Church, Karoly Tatray, a member of the Synod, expressed his deep gratitude to the Hungarian Government for its extraordinary cooperation.

"The Hungarian Peoples' Democracy has extended this same co-operative policy toward the Catholic Church. It is not our fault that these efforts have been in vain."

At this point one of the members of Parliament of the Barankovics Party shouted, "The government is wholly to blame."

"What is the explanation for this?" Dobi went on as if he had not heard. "It is this: that while the Hungarian Peoples' Democracy wishes and works for a desirable agreement Mindszenty and his clique do not want an agreement with the Popular Democratic state.

"Mindszenty's entire activity ever since the liberation has been designed to hinder the Hungarian Popular Democracy, not for religious but for political reasons. Popular Democracy has distributed the land of the big land

THE TIGHTENING OF THE NET 141

owners to the penniless peasants. Mindszenty is trying to take away the land from the new small holders and give it back to the big land owners."

At this point Ferenc Matheovics, of the Democratic Peoples Party, shouted, "That isn't true." And Ferenc Revesz of the Hungarian Workers Party (a Communist front organization) shouted back, "He said it himself, in his first pastoral letter." Joseph Revai also of the Hungarian Workers Party supported him with "Everything comes out at last."

Dobi went on: "Hungarian democracy has taken the mines, the large factories, and the banks away from the capitalists and given them to the people. Mindszenty on the other hand is trying to take them back, robbing the people in order to give them again to the exploiting capitalists. Popular Democracy has created the independent Hungarian Republic but Mindszenty longs for the return of the Habsburgs and wishes to turn Hungary into a colony of the western imperialists. Hungarian democracy has punished the war criminals, has put a brake on the reactionaries and fascists and in the future will take still more energetic steps against them. But Mindszenty is the patron and organizer of fascists and war criminals. This is why he has so consistently refused to come to an agreement with democracy and why he has tried to form an illegal political party within the Catholic Church in opposition to the Peoples' Democracy.

"My government still wishes to come to an agreement with the Catholic Church but it has reached the conclusion that there is no prospect of any such agreement so long as Mindszenty is the head of the Church in Hungary.

That has also come to be realized by the masses of the people. During the last few weeks hundreds and thousands of telegrams have arrived at the government offices from many organizations who demand that we take severe measures against Mindszenty. Among these telegrams those which come from Catholic priests, congregations, religious university students and professors are constantly increasing."

Here Ferenc Matheovics again interrupted. "What kind of priests?" he asked. He was answered from the floor by two members of the Hungarian Workers Party, one of whom said, "Democratic priests," while the other, a woman, shouted, "Not from traitors. It would please you if all priests were fascists!"

When the noise had subsided Dobi went on: "This clearly shows that the Catholic people themselves recognize more and more clearly what a catastrophic policy Mindszenty is pursuing even from the point of view of the Church itself. It is understanding such as this which always brings about more and more support for the fight, not against religion and the Church, but against Mindszenty and his policy.

"My government is of the opinion that in this case we cannot ignore the wishes of the people. We wish to make it perfectly clear to both friends and enemies that those who have designs against the Popular Democracy are only running their heads against a wall. We wish to pursue a policy that even the blind may understand. Every hope for the restoration of the old reactionary regime is destined from the first to death. The hardness and intrepidity with which we proceed against the enemies of our people and

THE TIGHTENING OF THE NET 143

our democracy will be the standards of the love we feel towards that people and that democracy."

On December 17th one of Mindszenty's nieces who lives in Budapest wrote to another niece, living in New York, a letter in which she said of Mindszenty's mother:

"Aunt Barbara prays a great deal now and often weeps when she is alone. But when she is with the Cardinal she never cries. Aunt Barbara always puts her hand on the shoulder of the Cardinal."

XIV
"Now Men Are Needed"

THIRTY years ago I tried to tell the people of Hungary what justice was like in Soviet Russia, but my reports fell on deaf ears. It was as if I were speaking in a strange language which was unable to sway a naïve belief that people in authority could not act as I told them they were acting in Russia. The public was unable to understand that the words "morals," "government," "politics" and "justice" had quite different meanings in Bolshevik Russia from those which they had in the light of Hungary's thousand years of civilization. I remember especially how impossible it was for me to convince members of the lawyers' club in Budapest about the way trials were conducted in Communist Russia. My audience made up of judges, state prosecutors and private lawyers were so trained in the tradition that the function of the judge is to discover the truth and administer justice that they simply would not believe me when I said to them, "In Russia the court is now merely one of the regime's instruments of power. The Judge's duty there is to serve the regime by passing sentence as it dictates in order to strengthen it and to eliminate its enemies."

Bela Kun's regime in Hungary did not last long enough to establish the people's court firmly in the Russian manner, but Hungarians who were given no opportunity then to learn what Bolshevik court procedure was like have learned it well in the last three years. No case—at least no

"NOW MEN ARE NEEDED" 145

case involving a political offender—is actually decided independently in the court room on the basis of the free presentation of factual evidence there presented. The decisions have been made before the case comes to trial by the political leaders assigned to this task and the sentence dictated to the judge before the trial begins. The inquiry, the evidence presented in the court room, are only parts of a grim farce carefully prepared before hand in order to support the sentence which has already been decided. These keep up appearances and help to establish the fiction that the country is still ruled by the processes of law.

So accustomed are the Communists to this procedure that they grow careless and make naïve blunders which instantly reveal their method to any intelligent observer.

In the "Yellow Book" published by the Hungarian government in Budapest in January 1949, before the Mindszenty trial, and obviously prepared before the Cardinal's arrest, there are these two interesting statements. On page 88: "The above documents convincingly and undeniably justify the charges against Mindszenty, and the trial *that is soon to begin* (italics are mine) will cast light on every aspect of Mindszenty's list of crimes." This is a reasonable enough statement to make before a trial and seems simply to justify the Cardinal's arrest.

But on page 4 there is this statement: "The Hungarian government wishes to publish in this book a few of those many proofs it has at its disposal, the greater part of which are from Mindszenty's secret, buried files, which will prove tangibly and irrefutably to any unbiased man that Mindszenty and his company were guilty." To anyone who had not read the statement on page 88 or noticed the date on the book this would seem to be a statement made after the evidence had been presented to the court and Mindszenty had been found guilty and condemned. Indeed, he had been condemned before ever he was arrested.

Why do they take the trouble? Why don't they simply kill their victims without the expense and delay of a trial? As a matter of fact they do if the victim is obscure enough, if he is someone who can be disposed of without arousing the indignation of anyone except his near relatives and closest friends. But in the case of "big game" they feel obliged to follow the forms of conventional legal procedure. These people cannot disappear without widespread comment. In some cases (such as that of Mindszenty) the criticism would spread around the world. They feel it necessary to be able to say to the world, "We have given him a fair trial. You see we have followed conventional court procedure just as you do in your country."

And there is another reason for it; an occasional celebrated case such as that of Mindszenty, which will be discussed on every street corner and in every gathering in Hungary, is calculated to strike terror into the hearts of all opponents of the regime at home—perhaps even the more because the Hungarians now know how false the entire procedure is and that the final sentence is inevitable.

Meanwhile they publicly admit the purpose of their court procedure. At the height of the discussion about the Mindszenty affair in Hungary, *Hirlap* made this comment: "Karoly Nagy, the new president of the civil court of Budapest, was installed on Saturday. At the meeting of the court, Istvan Riesz, Minister of Justice, made a speech in which he declared that the ideological re-orientation of the judges' corporation was of great importance. 'We do not deny,' he declared, 'that jurisprudence is one of the weapons of the class fight. We must do our best to make it a sharper weapon than ever.'"

This is exactly the principle expressed by Vishinsky during the trials of Tukhachevsky, Bukarin, Kamenev and Zinoviev, at which time he was State prosecutor: "The court is the instrument of politics."

The duties of the State prosecutor, the State investigators and the judge behind the Iron Curtain in cases against political offenders are clearly defined. They are simply to prove the guilt of the accused by every means at their disposal; false testimonies, false documents and false confessions obtained by the most brutal and effective methods must be produced when necessary. All means which support a seeming justification for conviction are good means. There are no illegal methods save those which do not produce the desired results.

The methods vary with the political importance of the victim and the specific aim of the Party in each case. The simplest and most brutal tortures are used in cases in which the accused are of minor political importance. Such cases are often the result of personal jealousies, the resentments of party members, or in local politics, the desire to get a troublesome person out of the way. Every country behind the Iron Curtain knows of many such cases. Indeed, the Communists have no desire to suppress this knowledge. It helps to maintain the atmosphere of dull terror which is so helpful to their regime.

The case of a former police official, for instance, was known to everyone in Hungary. Let us call the two men involved by names which are easier for English-speaking people, than are their real names, which do not matter. Let us call them Smith and Brown. Brown had been a petty thief and before the war, Smith, a detective, had arrested him and brought him to conviction and punishment. When the Communist regime came in Brown joined the Party and was rewarded by being made a police officer. He promptly arrested Smith for no crime whatever and brought him to the dreaded headquarters of the secret police at 60 Andrassy Street in Budapest. After several days' confinement in a darkened room, he was led into a room where the windows were covered with thick blankets. Here three men came to him and without any words began to beat him. Since he was an exceptionally strong man, he defended himself most creditably and re-inforcements were called in. Soon he was overpowered, stripped, and bound to rings on the wall where his real torture began under the leadership of a sadistic woman, one of those who are especially trained by the secret police to administer tortures, an accurate description of which would be almost unprintable. Thus Brown had his revenge for the arrest and punishment he had so richly deserved. Smith eventually escaped and was able to tell his story.

Cases of this kind are very common, and now after the first years of futile indignation and resistance are almost apathetically accepted by the public.

The methods used in cases of major political importance are less well known even to those who are behind the Iron Curtain. A thick veil of secrecy is deliberately let down to conceal them. The Communist policy in Hungary tries in such cases to keep up the appearance of adhering to the liberal Hungarian criminal code of 1875, a fine piece of legislation with full guarantee of the civil rights of the accused. Here the Communists have a difficult task. Their trials must convince public opinion, especially abroad, that the accused has been given a fair trial and at the same time they must make sure both that they condemn the leader of a hostile group, and terrorize his followers. Hungarian Communist prosecutors, as did their Nazi predecessors, seldom fail to call to the attention of the judges the fact that not only are the defendants on trial but that the movement or group which they represent is also.

Every member of the court personnel, judges, prosecutors and even defense attorneys has been carefully schooled by experts from Moscow in the conduct of trials. While the general pretense of following the criminal code of 1875 is kept alive any defense lawyer who quotes clauses from it guaranteeing the rights of the accused will quickly find himself removed from the bar. Trials are conducted in small rooms which make it very simple to exclude unwanted witnesses. Broadcasts of trials are used to lend a greater appearance of legality but they are quickly cut when unwanted evidence is unexpectedly spoken in court. And last but not least, there is the almost inevitable "confession" of the accused which has been obtained by the most subtle methods of torture which have ever been known to man. Since under Hungarian law the prosecutor must prove the guilt of the defendant even though he has pleaded guilty, the confession is relied upon to fulfill this requirement under any circumstances, and the Communists have found that there are ways to make practically anyone confess to practically anything.

The cast of Mr. B., the details of which I know personally as facts, is typical. Charged with conspiracy he was put into a wet and cold underground cell on starvation rations and left there alone without questioning for over a week. Then in the middle of the night, he was awakened and led from the freezing cold of his solitary cell to the bright and well-heated room of the interrogator. Here he was treated most courteously and asked to make a confession, being told that a friend and colleague had already confessed the whole matter so that his statement would be merely a matter of form. When he said that he had no confession to make, he was led back to the darkened, cold solitude of the cell.

After several more days of freezing and thin soup, he was again interrogated, this time by two men who overwhelmed him with alternate questions and threats and who after awhile were replaced by two other men. This system of replacement and of questioning kept on for what Mr. B. later estimated to be two days and two nights during which he was constantly kept awake and under questioning without food and without rest. During all this time he sat in the glare of a bright light which shone directly into his eyes. Finally he became completely exhausted so that he was almost unable to speak.

Then he was led or carried into another room and made to stand until he collapsed. After he was revived he was made to sit at a table and to write a long report of his political activities.

"NOW MEN ARE NEEDED"

A few days later he was again brought up for interrogation and was shown the statement he himself had written. Now he found that in his exhaustion, when he wanted to consider some point of importance or avoid the mention of the name of an acquaintance, he had written the same word over and over and over again. He said later that it seemed as if his body and soul had become disconnected and that his body had become simply an automatic machine.

Apparently his statement was unsatisfactory because the interrogation was carried on again for a very long time. Frequently it was stopped and he was beaten by guards. They beat the soles of his feet, his shin bones, and his knees, concentrating on the latter and increasing the pain by making him kneel repeatedly. Between the interrogations, highly trained members of the Communist Party came in and gave him long lectures, proving his guilt and trying to increase the psychological burden imposed upon him by a realization of the failure of the policies he had helped to form. Finally he was completely broken down and confessed to everything which his interrogators dictated to him. When he appeared in court, he had the appearance of a man under hypnosis. Later his confession was used to break down the resistance of his co-defendant.

When Mr. B. was finally set free, his friends asked him why he had confessed to so many things which he quite obviously could not have done.

"There was a period," he declared, "when I believed that I had done everything they told me I had done."

Other defendants undergo less elaborate preparations. Another whose case I know personally, a county secretary of the Hungarian Peasants Union, was arrested and almost immediately was subjected to the crudest and cruelest forms of physical torture, including the slow smashing of his finger bones one by one. Another was exposed for weeks to threats that he or his family would be deported to Russia. When these threats did not accomplish their object, he too was subjected to alternate questioning and beatings, until finally he signed the confession they demanded.

Ordinarily drugs are not used except in cases of unusual resistance to the other methods. Apparently the drug used is aktedron, a stimulant (which seems to be similar to benzedrine) which in large doses produces unusual mental alertness followed by complete exhaustion and apathy. After the development of this drug in Hungary in 1935, eighty percent of the Hungarian supply was exported to Russia.

Only a very few cases are known in which men of exceptionally strong mental resistance have withstood the methods of the police. Most of such cases never can be known since the victims usually die under the treatment if it does not produce the desired effect. Mr. Emery Veer, a member of the Hungarian Parliament of 1945 and of the Paris League of Human Rights, stated in a meeting of the Small Holders' Party in January 1946, that up to that time less than a year after the Communists had come into power, there had come to his attention 64 cases in which the victims of the secret police had died under torture.

One famous case, this time of a man who got away, is that of Dr. Zoltan Nyisztor, domestic prelate of His Holiness Pius XII. The following is his statement made under oath at Bogota after he had escaped:

"I was arrested by the Russians toward the end of November 1946 and taken to a villa on the outskirts of Budapest. I was questioned the same day, and an officer of the NKVD declared that I was accused of anti-Communist activities and of having published articles attacking the Red Army. He added that I was thereby subject to capital punishment or deportation to Siberia, but explained later that I could avoid this by 'offering my services' to the Red Army. I replied immediately that I refused to do this.

"I was then placed in a dismantled bathroom with the obvious purpose of breaking down my resistance. There was nothing in the room except a table, a bench and a board on the cement floor on which to lie down. By that time winter had arrived in all its fierceness and the thermometer had dropped to between 10 and 15 degrees below zero centigrade. I spent 20 days in this dismal atmosphere. My daily food ration consisted of two plates of soup, a cup of Russian tea and a small piece of bread. Opportunity for the exercise of physical functions was given me only once a day. The two woolen blankets I had, proved insufficient for warding off the bitter cold. During the night, drunken guards kept me constantly awake, so that I seldom managed to get any sleep.

"The meager rations, the biting cold, the prolonged questioning, always held at night, the constant menace of death, the lack of sleep, the dreary outlook, the terrible moanings of the victims in the torture chambers, the fear that my turn would come next, all this coupled with my previous six months' imprisonment in a Hungarian jail, had exhausted me to such a point that I had become emaciated. I was so weak, that during the last days I could lie down and rise only with great effort or with the help of the guards.

"On the 20th day I was again taken out for questioning. My wretched appearance impressed the Russian officer who, with an ostentatious show of sympathy offered me a seat, inquired about my health and gave me a cigarette. He then proceeded to explain at length how I was wrong in believing that the services required of me in exchange for my freedom were denunciations, espionage, or the like.

" 'Nothing of the sort!' he said. 'All we want is unbiased information about Hungarian affairs, which no one better than you can supply.'

"Although the meaning of his words was clear to me, I decided after due consideration to play a double hand in order to mislead them and save my own life at the same time. During the previous interviews I had realized that I was dealing not with respectable enemies, but with debauched criminals, vulgar executioners, the scum of humanity, and concluded that not even martyrdom was worth accepting from their hands. Furthermore I saw that all these officers were so illiterate, gullible and even childish, that it would not be a difficult task to deceive them.

"I therefore accepted the obligation of rendering the information I could obtain and was set free within a few days. Two weeks later I was called upon to make my

"NOW MEN ARE NEEDED" 155

reports and thereafter I was called every week. I had no difficulty with the first reports. The questions were chiefly concerned with the problem of Legitimism and the social and university movements. My method in answering them consisted in making these movements appear harmless and irrelevant, while I described the persons involved as ignorant, insignificant and of no importance.

"But the questioning gradually centered more and more upon Cardinal Mindszenty. They wanted me to discover who were employed in his service, what role each one played, how much influence each had, which were conscious of his plans or were admitted into his confidence. Although they referred to him with a carefully simulated respect, they unconsciously revealed by some of their remarks, that they considered him as their only powerful adversary, and their fiendish plans were soon clear to me. They were conspiring to weave a spy-net about him, to control his every movement and trap him later on. I received the impression that there were already several priests and aids of the Cardinal involved in the spy-net being drawn about him by the Russians.

"From then on my double role became more difficult. They became less and less satisfied with my elusive answers and insisted upon my visiting the Cardinal, who had just returned from Rome. I arranged things so that the Cardinal could not receive me and was then ordered to go to his residence in Esztergom to discover with whom he had established contacts while in Italy.

"My conscience was relieved when I discovered that I could not bring myself to obey any longer, and I decided to escape immediately. Unfortunately the car placed at my disposal by Msgr. Bela Varga broke down at the last moment and my plan to escape failed.

"Apparently complying with Russian orders, I went to Esztergom. The Cardinal gave me a warm and hearty reception but instead of trying to obtain any information from him I confided my unswerving resolution to escape from the country. To please the Russians I brought them a report of the Cardinal's trip written by himself which was published several days later in a Catholic weekly. The gullible Russians were quite satisfied until they saw my report in print. Then they were furious and attempted to intimidate me with terrible threats. It looked as if they would never let me go out again and that my end would soon come.

"Fortunately a sermon by the Cardinal was scheduled for the following day in the Basilica of Budapest and for this reason I was ordered 'as a final test' to assist at the sermon and reveal its contents to them immediately afterwards.

"Once on the street again I made sure I was not being followed. I then changed my course and, instead of going home, took refuge in the house of a close friend from where, many weeks later and again with the kind assistance of Msgr. Bela Varga, I succeeded in escaping in disguise and crossed the border."

This was the general situation which Cardinal Mindszenty faced in Hungary in 1948. At any time up to the day of his arrest, he could have left and found asylum in Rome, England, France, America—anywhere on the other side of the Iron Curtain. The Communists would not have prevented his going—indeed they would have welcomed it. It would have been a simple solution for them of the Mindszenty dilemma. But as he had often said to others, he now doubtless said to himself, "Now men are needed here."

XV
Time Runs Out

THERE was no doubt in Mindszenty's mind as to his eventual arrest, imprisonment, and perhaps death, at the hands of the Communists. The only question was when it would happen. He wanted his position to be made clear to his people. In his last pastoral letter, issued at Esztergom in November, 1948, he wrote:

"For weeks so-called 'charges' have been made against me in the various localities of dismembered Hungary. My accusers condemn the 'counter-revolution and acts committed against the people' fomented by me during the Days of the Holy Virgin which were celebrated in the various centers of the country during 1947 and 1948. They complain about the lack of an understanding between Church and State. They insist upon putting a stop to my 'detrimental activities.'

"The purpose of the Days of the Holy Virgin as part of the year of the Holy Virgin is the deepening of the traditional adoration of the Virgin and the strengthening of religious consciousness. Never did any question of a political nature arise during those Days. On the contrary, we proclaimed, in addition to the virtues and adoration of the Holy Virgin, the Ten Commandments, human dignity, brotherly love, and truth.

"It is wanton play with the public interest to force depositions from people upon threat of loss of their daily bread and personal freedom, while the rest of the country is damned to silence and driven from the ramparts of constitutional self-government. Democratic freedom of speech is here distorted in such a way that objections are either ruled out or, if attempted (as outstanding examples show), entail the loss of a job or other interference. The sufferings of those who have attempted to object pains me deeply. All my sympathy goes to those who are the victims of force. I am moved by the beautiful examples of moral strength and faithfulness which they have set.

"Regarding my alleged 'offenses' I am still without explanation. I have asked that the government make my letters public. This has not been done. My accusers prefer to cling to foggy generalities.

"The reason that there is no accord between Church and State or—more properly—between Church and the Party is, as everyone knows, the fact that the invitation to the discussions of such an accord arrived three months late and simultaneously with the government taking unilateral action on the main subject of the accord, namely, religious education. The role of the scapegoat was, of course, again assigned to the Church.

"I am still facing calmly the artificially whipped up waves. Around the rock where I stand guarded by grace and the trust of the Holy See, the raging tides of history are not unknown. Two of my predecessors fell on the field of honor. Two others had all their possessions confiscated. John Vitez was thrown into prison. Martinuzzi was assassinated by the hirelings of the mighty. Pazmany, the greatest of them all, was banished. Ambrus Karoly fell a victim to contagious disease while visiting and tending the sick.

But none of my predecessors were so without means of defense as I am. All seventy-eight of them together were not compelled to face so many purposely contrived and a hundred times denied, but stubbornly repeated, untruths as I am.

"I stand for God, Church, and my country. This historic duty is bestowed upon me by the service of my people— the most orphaned people in all the world. When compared to the sufferings of my country, my own fate is unimportant.

"I am not accusing my accusers. If, from time to time, I must cast a light upon conditions, it is only a revelation of my country's surging pain, its welling tears, its truth crucified. I pray for a world of justice and brotherly love; I pray for those, too, who, in the words of my Master, know not what they do. I forgive them with all my heart."

No one knew better than Mindszenty what went on at 60 Andrassy Street to which he knew he would be taken after his arrest. All of Hungary's complaints during these days had found their way to him. He had talked personally with many of the victims of the NKVD who had later been released.

He knew the secrets of the rubber-padded cells. He knew how victims were made to stand upright with faces turned to the wall for hours, and sometimes for days, until they collapsed. He knew how they were made to drink salt water. He knew how they were starved for days and then made to watch while others feasted. He knew the effect of hours of staring into strong electric lights, of short-wave electrical treatment, and of the use of drugs.

TIME RUNS OUT 161

He knew of the dead bodies which were secretly carried by night out of 60 Andrassy Street.

He knew the story of the famous wrestler who during the first days of his imprisonment shook off his torturers as a Carpathian bear would shake off dogs and how the same man, a few days later, became a puppet in the hands of his torturers and a spy for the NKVD. He knew how one of the best-known representatives of Catholicism had been forced to spy upon him and how he had confessed his sin upon his knees before a fellow priest and then been helped across the border.

Dr. Joseph Jaszovszky, archiepiscopal councillor and manager of the Hungarian Catholic Peoples League, had told him his story, a story which was later repeated in the statement which follows:

"Near the end of September in 1947 two members of the secret police appeared in my office and said to me, 'Do you know, sir, that every night people disappear in Hungary and that tonight it may be you?'

"I told them that I was quite aware of the situation, and they told me that nothing would happen to me if I would sign a statement in the name of the Catholic Peoples League concerning the activities of Cardinal Mindszenty, if I promised to remove certain people from the league, if I confirmed the declarations of the police against Mindszenty, and finally if I were willing to give the police day-to-day information about the bishops who surrounded the Cardinal.

"When I energetically refused to accept this proposal the police locked the door and threatened to arrest me at once. Apparently, however, they decided that my arrest at that time would cause too much excitement. They spent four hours trying by threats and persuasion to make me agree and finally left saying that their Commandant would come to see me, and threatened me with death if I told anyone about their visit.

"As soon as possible I made a detailed report of the conversation to Cardinal Mindszenty. After this I tried to avoid the police but during the next few weeks I was subjected to ten interrogations. During these the police officers reviewed all their charges against Mindszenty, especially emphasizing their accusation that the Cardinal was in continuous contact with Archduke Otto of Habsburg and was conspiring to return him to the Hungarian throne. They said that they had copies of the Cardinal's entire correspondence with the Archduke.

"In July, 1948, I was given a positive order to certify to the accusations against the Cardinal. I went into hiding and in October finally succeeded in escaping the country."

Shortly before his arrest three men were sent to Mindszenty by the Hungarian government in a final atempt to obtain his compliance—Zoltan Kodaly, the famous composer who, with Bela Bartok, has founded a new school of modern music in Hungary, Joseph Cavallier, a Catholic journalist and before the war an honest man and Gyula Szegfu, one of the most despicable figures of Hungarian political life who had been a university professor, and with quick opportunism had quickly entered the cause of the Russians when they arrived.

After this visit Mindszenty knew that his time was short.

It was about this time that he made his now famous declaration before the conference of Hungarian bishops: "I have taken part in no conspiracy whatsoever. I do not wish to confess anything to those who accuse me. I have no statement to sign. In case I do make a confession it will be only a manifestation of human weakness."

Now the government put on its final act of preparation for the Cardinal's arrest by spreading a wave of terror across the country directed especially toward the clergy and ecclesiastical institutions. In Budapest, in Vac, in Ajka, in Nyiregyhaza, in Kalocsa, in Szolnok, in Debrecen, in Szentes, in Pecs, in Miskolc and in hundreds of other cities and villages people were ordered into the streets for mass demonstrations. Students, apprentices, police employees, and Party functionaries marched through the main streets singing revolutionary songs, then went to the local parish buildings and presented demands that the priests stop the public reading of the Cardinal's pastoral letters and at the same time sign a statement repudiating the Cardinal. In some places the leaders of the organized mobs were so menacing that priests, in panic, fulfilled their demands. By far the majority, however, stood their ground, refusing, and rebuking the terrorists.

When Christmas arrived everyone in Budapest knew that the days of the Cardinal were numbered. The Hungarian newspaper *Uj Ember* reported: "The pilgrimage of believers to midnight mass surpassed in number any in memory. In Pest and Buda the streets were crowded long before midnight. Such crowds took part at the masses that everywhere they overflowed the churches and clustered around them in the nearby streets and squares. In many places near the churches, people knelt on the pavements, even between the rails of the tramways, praying."

It was no accident that the Communists chose Cardinal Mindszenty of Hungary as their most striking example. It is a reflection of the fact that they have encountered unusual difficulties in gaining full cooperation from Hungarian peasants and workers. This is also evidenced by the fact that, whereas in other countries of eastern Europe, under Russian domination, the Governments quickly threw away their masks and allowed themselves to be clearly revealed as made up of Communists, in Hungary there was a long and consistent attempt to keep up the appearances of a coalition government.

Look at the election figures. In 1945 the Communist Party received only seventeen percent of the votes—in 1947, even after using every fraudulent method they could conceive, they received only twenty-one percent. Not until after the 1947 elections were the opposition parties disbanded. Nowhere behind the Iron Curtain has there been more nearly complete and open oppisition to the Communist Party than in Hungary. Even among those who between 1945 and 1947 showed some Communist sympathies there are very many who have now turned against their masters. Realizing this, the Communists felt it unwise to stir the masses to more serious opposition by openly abandoning legal political forms and instituting clearly labeled Communist rule too soon and so the façade of a coalition government was kept long after Hungary was actually ruled by Communists.

And what did it really matter? The essential thing was

the maintenance of Party power. The Communists had the army, the political and economic police, and a highly trained skill in keeping fear alive. They used these weapons ruthlessly and effectively. Only during the reign of Bela Kun and during the Nazi occupation has such unrestrained terror ruled in Hungary as now.

Already the soundness of Mindszenty's opposition to the method of Hungarian land reform has been demonstrated. Actually, the giving of small pieces of land to individual peasants is in itself contradictory to Communist ideology. The Communists cannot tolerate independent existence which fosters independent thinking. Every individual must be forged into a part of the whole to follow dictated policy. In conformance with this standard the trend of the land reform has been exactly as Bela Varga told Mindszenty it would be. Hardly has the small farmer been given his land than it is taken away from him, always with the same explanation, that he does not produce enough and that what he does produce costs too much. This, of course, is the inevitable result of farming on very small holdings of land. The peasant cannot afford tractors, harvesting machines, threshing machines, cultivators, and fertilizers; even if he could mechanize his small farm such machinery as he could get could not be used efficiently and economically on such small holdings. Only the large estates or the collective farms are able to take full advantage of mechanization. The Communists' choice of course is the collective farm.

Actually, experience in Russia has shown conclusively that resentful peasants forced onto collective farms will, as a result of non-cooperation and sabotage, produce less than they do on independent small holdings. Nevertheless the government forces them into the collectives, for only thus can the peasants' independent existence be abolished, and that is the essential aim of the Communists.

Similar pressure has been brought to bear on the small business man. Shops have not been socialized but large State-owned department stores have been set up in competition with independent stores and regulations have been made which are slowly choking the individual tradesmen out of existence. He, too, is a menace, for he is an individualist. Not only is price competition used to eliminate him but the regulations for State-owned department stores and individually owned small shops are quite different. The department stores remain open from seven a.m. until eleven p.m., Sundays as well as week-days. The private shops may open only at nine a.m. and must close at five p.m., and remain closed all day on Sunday. Thus those who must go to work before nine and cannot return until after five cannot patronize the private shops at all. Further, the private shop is so heavily taxed that it is impossible for it to survive for long. Similar conditions are throttling the small privately owned factories. In Budapest alone from six to eight hundred licenses are allowed to lapse every month.

The fate of the intelligentsia is perhaps the most tragic of all. Teachers who wish to continue in their professions must join the Communist Party. If they do not consent they must leave their profession and are faced with starvation. Students are admitted to the universities only if they can prove that they are members of the Communist Party or bring recommendations from trade unions of their reliability as supporters of Communist doctrines. At such schools education in the best sense of the word no longer exists. In its place has been put Communist indoctrination.

Meanwhile hours of labor have become longer, wages insufficient and their purchasing power less and less because of rising costs. The right to strike has been abolished by the State, and the worker has been gradually sinking back to the level of existence which was his lot in the mid-nineteenth century, with one important difference. Then he was at least free to change his job and to move from one city to another. Today he can do neither. He may leave his factory only with the consent of his State-appointed superior. And he dare not complain. If he does so even slightly, he is forcibly transferred to another city, leaving his family and his accustomed living quarters behind him.

There is nothing which more clearly emphasizes the misery and discontent of the working class than the high percentage of workers among the refugees who daily cross the Austrian border seeking freedom in the west.

On December 10, 1948, my telephone rang in New York City and I cried out with joy when I recognized the voice of a friend whom I had last seen in Auschwitz. In 1944 we had been deported by the Nazis in the same railroad car. He is a powerful man with the build of a prize fighter. In the earliest days of Auschwitz he had intercepted many a blow which had been intended for me.

He had just arrived from Hungary. We met each other joyously and with tears in our eyes recalled many of our friends whose ashes had been scattered by the winds of Poland. Then we began talking about Budapest, our beloved home on the banks of the Danube, with its gayety, its glittering beauty and its Old World charm.

"Why did you come away, Gyula?" I asked.

"I couldn't stay," he answered sadly. "When I returned from Auschwitz I found everything in ruins. I was ill but I still had plenty of energy. I went to work but stayed strictly away from politics. I thought that if I worked peacefully, keeping out of politics, they would leave me in peace. But it didn't happen that way. At first they liquidated the political parties, then they began on all those peacefully engaged in private life. They started with the big estates, now they are taking away the small farm holdings. In business they started with the large enterprises. Now they are abolishing the small trades. The former middle class is almost entirely unemployed. Do you remember the excuse the Nazis used for taking away most of the people? It was because they had no jobs. And do you remember where they took them to? Auschwitz and the gas chambers. Do you remember when at the gypsy camp at Auschwitz in the pouring rain we first saw the yellow flames of the crematory in the sky? Thank you. One Auschwitz is enough for me."

There was none of this which Mindszenty did not know. There was none of it to which he was capable of giving anything except the most uncompromising opposition. But I am convinced that there was more behind the choice that he made than the mere desire to oppose the regime. And it is clear that he made a definite choice.

XVI

The Iron Hand
in the Rubber Glove

THE most trustworthy account which we have of Mindszenty's arrest and imprisonment up to the time of the trial comes from a Hungarian police official who was stationed at 60 Andrassy Street until January 15, 1949, when, unable longer to stand the things he was forced to see, and the duties which were assigned to him, he escaped to Austria. His statement follows:

"On the first day of Christmas the State Defense Authority ordered a strict readiness for its officers; even leaves had to be cancelled. Everybody had to report to 60 Andrassy Street. Here Lieutenant-Colonel Gyula Decsi told us that the time had come for finally settling the Mindszenty question. On December 26th a long line of motorcars started to Esztergom to arrest the Cardinal. The behavior of the Cardinal was formal and courageous. He bade farewell to his mother saying: 'Don't cry, Mother, your son will die for the freedom of our people.'

"Sixteen police officers [1] carried out Mindszenty's arrest. All were supplied with light automatic rifles. In Budapest the Cardinal was taken to the second floor of 60 Andrassy Street. This is the floor reserved for especially important prisoners.

[1] By a singular coincidence this is also the number of police officers used by the Nazis to arrest Mindszenty in 1944.

"During the first three days the Cardinal was treated politely and correctly. The quizzing began on the fourth day. Three interrogators took turns, each handing over his notes, as he was relieved, to the next. Lieutenant-Colonel Decsi led the quizzing in person and the first hearing took 82 hours without rest for Mindszenty. They did not beat him but he had to stand upright for the whole time. The Cardinal's first collapse came about when his most intimate collaborators [1] were brought before him weeping and covered with their own blood. His secretary, Andrew Zakar, had been frightfully tortured by the secret police. He was on the verge of madness and laughed hysterically at every question.

"'I'll say anything you want me to!' Zakar screamed repeatedly when he was again quizzed in Mindszenty's presence.

"On the fifth day of the quizzing Mindszenty became unconscious. The police doctor who was present brought him to with the 'stimulant pills' (probably aktedron) dissolved in water. The Cardinal's resistance broke and he gave the answers which his torturers wished to hear. It is a fact that the hand of Mindszenty wrote the confession which the Hungarian government published on the first page of the 'Yellow Book.' Up to that time when the pills given by the police completely broke his will, leaving him with a violent headache, total dullness and tormenting thirst, his resistance had been heroic. The police officers themselves called him their toughest case.

[1] There had also been arrested, to be tried with Mindszenty, his secretary, the Reverend Andrew Zakar, Prince Paul Esterhazy, the Reverend Miklos Nagy, the Reverend Bela Ispanky, and Lazlo Toth.

THE IRON HAND IN THE RUBBER GLOVE · 171

"Zakar, Prince Esterhazy and other collaborators of the Cardinal had at first been taken to a luxuriously furnished hotel at 10 Csokonay Street where for two days they lived undisturbed, though without food or drink. On the third day they were brought to the dungeon of 60 Andrassy Street. In these dungeons are 18 cells in each of which two to four persons are kept. The ordinary political delinquents are locked up in common cells; their bed is a board without either straw or blanket. The cells are unheated and moist and for the purpose of preparing the prisoners before quizzing they are locked up in solitary cells so low that they cannot stand up but must sit or crouch. From time to time most of the air is pumped out of each cell, leaving only enough so that the prisoner does not quite suffocate. Officers mark with chalk on the outside of the cell door the number of minutes that the air is to be drawn out.

"After this preparation Mindszenty's collaborators received the same stimulant pills as had been given to the Cardinal. In such a condition they were ready to sign any kind of confession in order to get back to their ordinary cells.

"The rubber-cell is used with exceptionally tough people. This is about as high as a man and is padded with rubber. The rubber-padding is filled with air. As soon as the prisoner enters the cell especially strong and brutal guards throw themselves upon him. These wear rubber gloves reaching to their shoulders. As the prisoner receives the first blow he flies against the rubber wall from which he flies back again and is beaten continuously. This kind of mishandling leaves no marks on the outside of the victim's body, but generally serious internal bleedings afterwards appear.

"Police officers who have especially distinguished themselves in these torture proceedings are Colonel Gyula Oszko and Major Andrew Csapo.

"The chief of the secret police at 60 Andrassy Street, Lieutenant-General Gabor Peter, works in an office, the ceiling of which has been painted at his wish with the moon and stars to simulate a nocturnal sky and create an atmosphere of infinite space and freedom. Even his closest assistants dare not pass the threshold of this sanctuary. They must slip their reports through the door. All leading officials at 60 Andrassy Street were trained in Moscow."

Another account of Mindszenty's arrest says that as they took him he turned to one of his priests and said, "If the living Cardinal cannot help his country and the world, perhaps the dead Cardinal can."

Now government propaganda turned to the task of convincing Hungary and the world of Mindszenty's guilt and the government's service in arresting and bringing him to trial.

The day after Mindszenty's arrest Father Koczan of Szombathely was ordered to appear at Communist headquarters. He was told of the Cardinal's removal from public life and asked whether he, Father Koczan, was prepared to co-operate "with Democracy." Substituting the word "Communism" for "Democracy" in his mind, Father Koczan said he would have to think it over.

Two nights later he was awakened and again taken to headquarters. This time he was shown a photograph of

THE IRON HAND IN THE RUBBER GLOVE 173

Andrew Zakar, the Cardinal's secretary, and Janos Fabian, an assistant (also under arrest) standing beside a long metal cylinder which they said contained the secret treasonable documents which would convict Mindszenty. They handed Koczan a statement denouncing the Cardinal for his "treasonable, underhanded activities." They said that it would be typed and that Koczan's signature must be the first to be affixed to it.

"Two friends will call for you Friday night," they said. "You will sign the statement and go with them to get the signatures of other priests. If you co-operate you will be made head of the Church in Hungary."

On Thursday night Father Koczan slipped across the border into Austria. "I left without giving them any satisfaction," he said in Vienna. "If I were younger and in better health, I might have defied him. But if I had stayed, I would not have survived."

On January 10, 1949, Sandor Barcs, a Communist spokesman, said in a broadcast from radio Budapest, "A dangerous cyst has been cut from the body of Hungarian democracy. Those who oppose this operation are enemies of the Hungarian people and of Hungarian Catholicism."

It was also in January that the government published at Budapest its famous "Yellow Book," to which I have already referred, most of which had obviously been prepared before his arrest. It is called *Documents on the Mindszenty Case* and the first document is the "confession" which the Cardinal was forced to sign in prison. In order to prove the authenticity of the confession a photographic reproduction of it in Mindszenty's handwriting is reproduced.

But the secret police made the rather stupid mistake of printing also photographic reproductions of certain letters which the Cardinal had written several months earlier. These latter written in the uninterrupted peace and seclusion of the Cardinal's palace at Esztergom reveal his habit of erasing or crossing out unsatisfactory words or phrases. Yet the "confession," written under the terrific strain of his imprisonment at 60 Andrassy Street, under the greatest physical and spiritual tension, contains not a single error. Not a word has been erased or changed; there is not a single correction of any kind in the entire document of 292 lines; though it is full of minor errors of spelling, the whole looks like a particularly praiseworthy exhibition of calligraphy.

As to the content it is fairly routine. It confesses the awful fact of the Cardinal's noble ancestry—that the Pehm family was declared noble in 1732 and that the Kovacs, his mother's family, were raised to the rank of nobility in 1663. It outlines briefly the history of his church career, freely acknowledges that he had always considered himself a royalist and that he had supported the monarchist movement and believed in a union between Hungary and Austria. He said that he expected the overthrow of the Hungarian republic with the help and support of other nations, chief of whom was the United States of America.

An interesting comment on the Hungarian Communists' attitude is contained in their treating the Cardinal's opposition to the Nazis as if that also were a crime against Hun-

THE IRON HAND IN THE RUBBER GLOVE 175

gary. On page 12 of the "Yellow Book" there is this strange statement, "Mindszenty himself admits his conflict with the Nazis." Then follows a clear statement of the Cardinal's arrest by Schiberna in October 1944.

But evidence of the bungling confusion of the trained propagandist's mind lies in the paragraph immediately following this which calls attention to "a characteristic proof of his sympathy for and interest in the cause of the Hungarian Hitlerites." The "proof" is a letter supposedly written by Mindszenty about Szalasi in 1938, six years before the Nazis entered Hungary.

Later, it is true, Szalasi became the president of the Arrow-Cross Party and in 1944 Prime Minister under the Nazis. Mindszenty's attitude toward him and his gang at this time is clearly revealed by a visit which the Cardinal made to the Prime Minister's office in Budapest on November 13, 1944, carrying a memorandum from the Trans-Danubian bishops to the Government protesting against Hungary's further prosecution of the war on the side of Germany. Because Szalasi happened to be absent that day he handed the memorandum to the Deputy Prime Minister Szollossy who, after reading it, entered into a violent dispute with the Cardinal.

"You gentlemen are the enemies of the Hungarian people," Szollossy said. "You are traitors to your country, trying to wrench the weapons of defense out of the hands of the nation."

"There are, to be sure, traitors," Mindszenty retorted, "but they are those who wish to continue the shedding of Hungarian blood for the lost cause of Hitler."

"This is defeatism and treason," the Deputy Prime Minister cried. "Does your Eminence know the fate of those who speak in this way?"

"Certainly," the Cardinal replied calmly, "prison, torture, the firing squad, or the gallows. I am a priest. I have already accepted this as my fate."

"Take care or you may get it," Szollossy said, and abruptly turning on his heel he left the room. This was the second time that a Prime Minister of Hungary had turned his back upon Mindszenty.

Needless to say the "Yellow Book" did not mention this meeting.

One of the paragraphs in the Mindszenty "confession" printed in the "Yellow Book" accused Joseph Kozi-Horvath, a high-ranking Catholic priest, of having sent reports to the Cardinal at the end of 1946 and the beginning of 1947 concerning his discussions of plans for the return of the monarchy with the Archduke Otto. The meeting between Otto and Kozi-Horvath supposedly took place December 12-14, 1946.

After the publication of the "Yellow Book" Kozi-Horvath in an interview with representatives of the French press in Paris, said, "That part of Cardinal Mindszenty's confession which refers to me is demonstrably completely untrue. At the times mentioned I was still behind the Iron Curtain in Soviet-occupied territory which I was quite unable to leave and the Archduke equally unable to enter. It was not until September 1, 1947 that I was able to cross the border and escape Russian jurisdiction. I met the Archduke for the first time in my life in August 1948. Previously I had no contact with him whatever, either in person or through correspond-

THE IRON HAND IN THE RUBBER GLOVE 177

ence. The 'confession' would be much more convincing if the Hungarian political police had reproduced the reports which they say I sent to the Cardinal. This they cannot do for the documents never existed."

Outside the prison the martyrdom of the Cardinal's mother, now 75 years old, was no less than his own. Throughout her life she had remained a simple, unassuming, humble woman whose habits of thrift and self-effacement did not change in any way as a result of her son's success. She supervised his household, mended and patched his clothing throughout his life as she had when he had been a little boy. It was a well-known fact among those who were close to Mindszenty that he wore darned socks and patched underwear and shirts until they would no longer hold together, and that his mother did all of his mending herself. At church she always sat (and still sits) in an inconspicuous pew towards the rear, refusing to make herself conspicuous by sitting forward.

Two years ago a journalist asked her when she had been the most happy.

"I've always been happy beside my son," she said. "I was happiest when I saw him prepare for the priesthood. Later I wept for him. I wept for him when he went to Veszprem as a bishop. I wept for him when they took him to Esztergom." Even then the wisdom of the mother foresaw the end.

How she must have wept for him during those days before the trial when her keen vision was able to pierce the walls of 60 Andrassy Street.

XVII
The Trial

PERHAPS the strangest of all the ironies of the Mindszenty trial is the fact that he was arrested, tried and convicted by former Nazis, men who had been members of the Hitler gang against whom the most violent vituperation in the Communist vocabulary had been uttered.

They were of course turn-coat Nazis, opportunists ready to join any powerful clique while it is in the ascendant in order to obtain power for themselves. The president of the People's Court, Dr. Vilmos Olti, had been a prominent member of the murderous Arrow-Cross Party and had served as judge under the Nazis as he does now under the Communists. He became a member of the Communist Party in 1945. The state official who led the investigation, now known as Dr. Martin Bodonyi, was assessor of the military tribunal under the Nazi regime. He then called himself Martin Schweitzer. He did not at once become a Communist when the Russians marched into Budapest but quickly succumbed to Communist pressure and is now a thoroughly "reliable" man by Communist standards. Most of the police officers who built up the case against Mindszenty are Hungarians of German ancestry.

Actually there is nothing surprising about this. There is no one whom the Communists welcome to the ranks of their police and courts with more eagerness than they do former Nazis. These men have already been thoroughly

THE TRIAL

trained in the Communists' own methods of coercion. They need much less schooling in the technique of torture and the distortion of truth than do ordinary decent or semi-decent citizens. Further, and especially in a country whose people hate Nazism as thoroughly as the people of Hungary do, there is always knowledge of their pasts to be used as a club; if they do not obey, their Nazi history can be dragged out and they can be exterminated with complete approval of the people.

It is a familiar saying among the Communists that "It isn't important who washes the dirty dishes. The thing that matters is that they get washed."

On the other hand the Communists shun like the plague all who resisted Nazism, knowing that these fighters for human liberty will resist the Communist oppressors as they did those from Germany.

Hungarian government and political life swarms with former Nazis. Sandor Schmidt, Nazi manager of one of the great coal companies, who was skilled by the Germans in torturing Jewish forced laborers, is now chief councillor for the coal mines. He knows how, by Nazi terroristic methods, to produce coal. Joseph Csikos-Nagy, a tool of the Nazis under German occupation, is now virtually the economic dictator of Hungary. When the Russians took over they imprisoned him as a Nazi. By torture they forced him to join the Communist Party. They now use his knowledge of business and banking for their own purposes.

Mindszenty knew whom he faced in the courtroom. He knew the records of all of these men. He knew that their evil ruthlessness was the same whether they called themselves Communists or Nazis. He knew that nothing which could be said in the courtroom would change his fate. He knew that his case was hopeless.

Yet he made one attempt to end the farce. The first sensation of the trial came when the President of the Court read aloud the following letter which Mindszenty had written to the Minister of Justice on January 29th:

"I ask the Minister of Justice to take my statement into consideration. It is my request.

"For some time charges have been made against me, that I injured the peace between the Church and the State by my hostile attitude towards the regime. Now I wish to lessen the present tension. In advance of the forthcoming trial, I voluntarily admit in principle that I am guilty of the activities with which I am charged, according to the State Criminal code. In the future I will judge the external and internal affairs of the Hungarian State on the basis of the sovereignty of the Hungary Republic.

"After this confession and statement, a trial of my person does not seem necessary. Therefore, and with regard not to my person but to my position, I request the withdrawal of my case from the trial of February 3rd. Such a decision would help a settlement much more even than a trial under the most advantageous conditions.

"After thirty-five days of constant meditation, I also declare that, partly because of other reasons, and partly because of my attitude as described above, an agreement was delayed. On the other hand, so long as it is not concluded, I consider an agreement between Church and State necessary. I will willingly take part in making such an agreement, according to the spirit and doctrines of the Church.

"To avoid the possibility of my person being an obstacle

THE TRIAL

to peace, and so that all energies may be devoted to the avoidance of technical obstacles, I hereby willingly declare, free from pressure, of course, that I am willing to withdraw from the exercise of my office for a time. If the majority of the Bench of Bishops decide that it would be beneficial to conclude an agreement, I would not oppose it. I also would not oppose the realization of a similar agreement with the Holy See, which has the last word in this case. I make this statement in the belief that both Church and State would benefit from a real peace. Otherwise, without peace, the country's life would be in danger.

"Cardinal Mindszenty, Archbishop."

Immediately the State prosecutor asked for the rejection of the request, the President of the Court rejected it, and the trial proceeded.

Mindszenty had chosen for his defense an old friend who was a member of Parliament and in whom he had full confidence, but the court would not accept him and assigned in his place Dr. Kalman Kiczko, who had been a member of the Communist Party since the days of Bela Kun in 1919.

At the opening of the trial Radio Budapest began its broadcasts from the courtroom with commentaries.

"We bring you a sound-picture of the Mindszenty criminals," the announcer thundered. "The traitor stands before his judges. The whole disreputable company, the representatives of counter-revolution and reaction are sitting in the dock. Joseph Pehm-Mindszenty, the high Church dignitary, unctuously referring to the teachings of Christ, tries to ruin the Hungarian people with murderous weapons wrapped in religious phrases. He has tried to take the land back from the peasants, the factories from the workers and to push the people back into the darkest misery. He has tried to make common causes with the decadent heir of a worn-out dynasty and with the agents of reaction in America. He has dealt illegally in currency and robbed the Hungarian State."

As with everything else at their disposal the Communists used the radio as an effective tool. Its use in the Mindszenty trial is typical. Beginning with an outright statement of the prisoner's guilt, it purported to broadcast the entire trial as an evidence that Communist trials are open and aboveboard, but throughout the proceedings there were several interruptions. If the accused or the witness happened to answer questions in a way that was awkward for the prosecution he was immediately cut off and the commentator began to put his remarks "in a correct light." There were six such breaks during Mindszenty's confession and one during Eszterhazy's. During the first day the Court sat from nine in the morning until nine-thirty in the evening but the broadcast from the courtroom included a total of only three hours of actual courtroom procedure.

Justin Baranyai, a university professor and president of of the Peoples Catholic League, was the first of the group to be questioned in Court.

"Do you feel guilty?" the president asked.

"No," Baranyai said calmly although he had previously signed a forced confession also.

Later it was disclosed that when his confession was placed before him by the police, he had said that he had signed it only as a result of complete exhaustion. Yet the truth in such cases is difficult to discover. It is well known that the Communists welcome occasional pleas of not

THE TRIAL

guilty from defendants of lesser importance, in order to demonstrate to the world the "freedom" and "justice" of their courtroom procedure.

The president asked him about the details of the Legitimist conspiracy. Baranyai denied that any such conspiracy existed or that there had been any plan to overthrow the Republic. He acknowledged, however, that his group had, discussed the possibility of a restoration of the monarchy in case a change came about through outside interference. During the time of foreign, probably American, occupation, he said, Mindszenty would probably have been chosen as temporary head of the State.

"With whom did you discuss your plan?" asked the president.

"I talked it over with Lipot Baranyai and I intended to forward a statement of it to the American Embassy, since we had in mind the possibility of an American victory and occupation in case of war."

Dr. Andrew Zakar was the next to be questioned. He began by saying that he felt guilty but not that he had done wrong ethically.

The president asked, "Did you know that Mindszenty wanted to seat Otto Habsburg upon the throne?"

"I knew about the Legitimist movement," Zakar answered, "but only from the outside. I knew for instance that the Cardinal received Legitimist visitors, among whom were Istvan Kray, Justin Baranyai, Count Cziraky, Margit Schlachta, and Miklos Gruber."

He was asked about Mindszenty's foreign journeys in connection with the alleged Habsburg conspiracy.

"Our first trip to Rome was on Nov. 30, 1945," he said.

"We went again in February 1946. On the second trip Mindszenty met the Belgian Cardinal van Roey who gave him a letter from Otto. This letter contained only brief greetings, respect and affection. The letter was destroyed by the Cardinal while he was still in Rome. Later, the Cardinal had further correspondence with van Roey concerning Otto Habsburg."

The president asked him about the journey which he made with the Cardinal to America and asked about his supposed meeting with Otto in Chicago in 1947. To this Zakar's reply was evasive. He said that they had met Cardinal Spellman in New York with whom Mindszenty had discussed Otto in Latin.

The "Yellow Book" which I have quoted several times previously had already printed the Communist version of the American meeting between Mindszenty and Otto in what were supposedly Mindszenty's own words. This version reported that Mindszenty had met Queen Zita at Ottawa during the Mary Congress in June 1947 and that early in July Mindszenty had gone to Chicago as a guest of Cardinal Stritch and that while there he had had a secret meeting at a nunnery at which his secretary was present. There, according to the "Yellow Book" statement, he had had an hour's talk with Otto and had received the Archduke's instructions that the monarchists should not form a separate party but work as quietly and with as little risk as possible, gaining parliamentary seats and other positions of authority in existing parties.

Actually, it has been stated unequivocally by those who were close to Cardinal Mindszenty during his American trip that at the time of his supposed visit with Otto in Chi-

THE TRIAL 185

cago he was actually in Ottawa and that he did not go to Chicago at all.

Zakar concluded his confession by saying that the Cardinal had asked for the intervention of the United States Army in Hungary and that he had had some little correspondence concerning this with both the United States and British Embassies in Budapest. He also said that Mindszenty had made a present of an automobile to the Vatican in exchange for the Vatican radio's establishment of a Hungarian news service.

This last was a strange reversal of the fact. There had indeed been a car exchanged between the Vatican and Mindszenty, but it had been in the other direction. Mindszenty's own car which he used constantly in his church and social work had become so dilapidated and unreliable that the Vatican had presented him with an Alfa-Romeo to enable him to carry out his duties with dignity.

Following Zakar's testimony, Mindszenty was called to the bar. When asked by the president whether he felt guilty, he answered clearly, "Insofar as I have done a number of the things with which I am charged and as I noted in my letter to the Minister of Justice, I do feel guilty—"

At this point the radio transmission was abruptly cut off. Quite obviously the Cardinal's carefully thought out answer was not quite according to plan. It is easy to see his dilemma here. If he were to say at this point that he did not feel guilty it would be to deny his opposition to the Communist regime and his attempts to help save Hungary. Plainly he had counted upon using the radio through which the trial was being broadcast to reassert in carefully chosen statements his most deeply held political convictions, but with an easy flip of a little switch a radio operator prevented this.

When transmission began again the president was asking about his relations with Archduke Otto. Mindszenty said that he had received the first message from the Archduke in 1945 by way of the Marquis Pallavicini and that this message urged him to work secretly.

He was then questioned about the role played in the conspiracy by Kozi-Horvath and it was at this point that he made the statement that the latter, then in France, had sent him messages from Otto in 1946. This statement, as Kozi-Horvath showed, was false.

The president himself then discussed a part of the contents of the confession Mindszenty had signed in prison. According to this, Kozi-Horvath had discussed in his letters to Mindszenty negotiations which had been carried on with Croatian, Slovenian, Ukrainian, Slovakian and Austrian Legitimists and reported secret preparations which were being made for a third world war. These letters, according to the president, stressed the fact that one could not leave everything to the big powers but that the anti-Communist forces of the countries behind the Iron Curtain must organize under the anti-Bolshevik banner of Christianity.

Mindszenty: Yes, these were the contents of the letters.

President: How could you imagine the possibility of a restoration of the monarchy? In the spring of 1947 the Republic was already two years old and had grown strong.

Mindszenty: We thought of it only in the event of an historic change coming from the outside.

President: Could you not see clearly that the masses of

THE TRIAL 187

the people here do not want the restoration of a Habsburg?

Mindszenty: We did not want any revolutionary activities. We felt that it might come about through an historic event. We made no moves whatever from the inside.

The president then called attention to the fact that Mindszenty was charged with having asked for American intervention. Mindszenty then made the following statement:

"I accept these proofs as I have stated before and acknowledge having sent some of these documents, which I regret. These documents were divided into three parts. The first group, the smaller and least important, were ready and addressed but were not sent off. The greater part was delivered. Their purpose was not to accuse anyone but only to help. The purpose was right but the way I did it was wrong. It would be better if I had never sent the letters. In the future I shall consider the affairs of the Hungarian State the affairs of the Government."

It is obvious that the broadcast of this statement was cut, for in the beginning Mindszenty mentions three groups of letters and the radio mentioned only two. We have an interesting report on the third group from the *Basler Nachrichten*. According to this report this group includes letters which Mindszenty had really mailed and which told of the terrible conditions imposed by the Communists upon Hungarian prisoners of war, Hungarian minorities in Czecho-Slovakia, and similar groups. "I sent these to foreign powers," the Cardinal said, "and I do not regret it. For these were within my pastoral function and were written for the purpose of giving needed help." But this statement was carefully eliminated from the broadcast.

The president then returned to the subject of the monarchist conspiracy and asked whether plans for the restoration of Otto did not meet with the approval of certain powerful groups in America. Mindszenty answered that they did. The president then showed him the Archduke's denial of having met Mindszenty in Chicago which was published in foreign papers, and the Cardinal made no comment.

Questioned as to whether he had given information concerning conditions in Hungary to the American Minister, Selden Chapin, Mindszenty said that he had.

"What kind of information did you give him?" the president asked. "Did you praise the conditions here?"

"On the contrary," Mindszenty answered.

The president mentioned one of Chapin's visits to Esztergom and asked whether the Minister had offered to help Mindszenty escape abroad.

Mindszenty: This thought was far from him.

President: Do not answer in such a round-about way. Say yes or no. Did Minister Chapin offer to help you to escape?

Mindszenty, in a trembling voice: Must I answer this?

President: You do not have to answer anything but if you do not answer you deprive yourself of the possibility of defense.

Mindszenty: Yes, he offered to help me escape.

The trial of the others proceeded quickly. Miklos Nagy and Bela Ispanky confessed espionage and provided a

THE TRIAL

grimly amusing moment when the State prosecutor said, "It is forbidden to spy for either England or America." The president quickly corrected him by interposing, "It is forbidden to spy for any country."

Dr. Laszlo Toth started his statement with an hysterical outbreak reminiscent of the Moscow trials.

"I am guilty," he cried. "I have committed a crime. Now I must answer for it."

During the entire trial Mindszenty maintained a remarkable composure, but the drawn, strained look on his face and the almost glazed apathy of his eyes, broken only occasionally by flashes of righteous anger, bore awful testimony to the ordeal of questioning and drugging to which he had been submitted while in prison awaiting trial. Another of the mistakes which the Communists made was to allow his picture to be taken in the courtroom and published. To those who knew him or even to those who had seen former pictures of him, the shocking difference between the courtroom pictures and his normal appearance, was a more graphic evidence of the torture to which he had been subjected than any statement could have been.

Another surprise came in the trial when State Prosecutor Gyula Alapi read a letter alleged to have been written in prison by Cardinal Mindszenty on January 23rd, and exhibited it to prove that it was in Mindszenty's handwriting. It was addressed to Selden Chapin, the American Minister, and said:

"Mr. Minister: Something must be done before Thursday and I ask you to do it, for a sentence has already been decided on and the trial is so planned as to implicate the United States of America. My accusers are trying to prove that I have received money from America in exchange for official secrets. I ask that you obtain a car and a plane for me. There is no other solution. Promise the pilot $4,000 which I shall pay."

Recently American handwriting experts, having carefully examined a photographic copy of this letter along with specimens of Mindszenty's handwriting, have said that the letter is a very skillful fraud having obviously been written by a very clever handwriting expert.

In his summing-up speech for the prosecution Alapi emphasized the Government's position that the trial in no way reflected a policy of religious persecution but was intended merely to bring a traitor and enemy of the State to justice.

"There is not a country in the world," he said, "whose laws would not justify the heaviest punishment for the crimes of the defendants. Hungarian democracy has the same right to proceed against its enemies as has any other form of government. I, as prosecutor, would be guilty of betraying my office if I did not proceed according to this conviction. Not one of the defendants has denied the validity of the documents presented in evidence against them. They have plotted against the republic. They are spies. In deciding upon a verdict, the court must take into consideration the fact that Mindszenty's position makes his guilt even heavier than that of the others, since by making the Church appear as an enemy of the Republic he casts suspicion on Catholicism itself."

He then attempted to implicate the American Government and American Catholicism.

"Mindszenty asked Chapin for help and Chapin prom-

THE TRIAL 191

ised it to him," he said. "The idea that Cardinal Mindszenty should authorize Archduke Otto to represent Hungarian Catholics abroad was conceived by Cardinal Spellman."

In closing he asked the court to impose the maximum penalty upon the Cardinal, saying, "The verdict should be a hard-hitting example."

The summing up of the defense attorney, Dr. Kalman Kiczko, was a travesty of defense. He completely agreed that the defendant had harmed the popular Democracy, pointing out that the Cardinal himself had admitted it. He repeated in substance Alapi's statement that there was no question here of the persecution of religion, saying that in Hungary the freedom of religion was not in any way being questioned or under attack. He spoke at some length about the attitude of the Church toward land reform, pointing out that the Church itself was a large land holder although its possession of the land was not founded on justice. He made a gesture toward calling attention to an extenuating circumstance by saying that the Cardinal, regardless of his own convictions, was of course completely subject to orders from the Vatican. He spoke in much the same sense about Mindszenty's attitude toward State education.

"One might say," he went on, "that the defendant, in the dignified solitude of a primate's existence, lived in an ivory tower and was incapable of understanding the inevitable course of historical development. That the defendant has admitted his guilt is a gain for popular Democracy which is now being accused in many parts of the world. In many places it is being charged that religion is persecuted in Hungary. Now that this trial has taken place those who have accused us falsely can see clearly the spirit of free inquiry which has ruled here; they can see our freedom of defense in action, and learn that the defendants have been condemned by their own consciences. The charges of our accusers have collapsed. The malevolence of the accusers themselves has been proved." He ended his speech with a statement in praise and support of the nationalization of schools.

In Hungarian law the accused has the right of the last word at his trial. Taking advantage of this, Mindszenty made a long statement, apparently in a tremendous effort to force his mind and his speech to rise above the confusion and apathy which drugs had forced upon it. Yet it remains a confused statement.

"Exercising the right of the last word," he said, "a man stands before the court in a position of high responsibility and weighed down with charges.

"I stand here with the education and basic principles acquired in over half a century of living, principles which are built into the human soul as railway lines are built on the earth, and which are used to keep us in a straight direction as the rail keeps the train.

"Now I stand before the police authorities and the court, faced by questions and answers which enlighten not only the authorities but also the soul. Examining the answers I have given myself I thank God that at no time in the course of my life have I lost my good will. I have never wanted to come into conflict with the law. If circumstances beyond my control have brought me into such conflict I have confessed and regretted it.

"Secondly, I thank God that I have not been and am not

THE TRIAL

now an enemy of the Hungarian people. I have never had any trouble with the Hungarian worker or the Hungarian farmer, a class to which my family belongs. I have not wanted to take away from any social class any right that belonged to it.

"After the second World War, I had to play a very difficult historical role. I was supposed to be the preacher of the light and love of the gospel.

"On several occasions the question of land reform and the relation of the Church to the State have been discussed here. Therefore I must mention in passing that in May, 1945, the Board of Bishops in their pastoral letter sent their blessing to those who had newly become land owners under the land reform. On four occasions the Board made declaration that it did not ask that the land be taken from the diligent small land owners who deserve it. The Vatican has never disapproved of this declaration.

"I thank God that, in my own investigation of my severe conscience, I have found no evidence that I have ever been an enemy of the people. I have never been against peace between the Church and the State but have only demanded conditions under which it would be a lasting peace.

"My present point of view is reflected in the letter which I wrote to the Ministry of Justice on January 29th. It has been read in this court. I maintain this point of view.

"I have confessed that, due to circumstances beyond my control, I have come into conflict with the law. I have offered to pay for any financial damage I have done.

"This morning the following prayer came to my lips:

God give us peace in these days, not merely in the future, but in these days. I ask this peace for my Church, my love for which is constantly with me, for the Hungarian State to which I have shown my obedience, and for my own soul. I ask the Lord to give the court the wisdom to arrive at a sentence which will guarantee a solution both here and abroad."

The court adjourned for two days; it then reconvened and sentenced Cardinal Mindszenty to imprisonment for life.

Immediately, throughout the still articulate countries of the world, the voice of protest arose.

In New York's St. Patrick's Cathedral on February 6, before the sentence had been pronounced, Cardinal Spellman delivered a sermon completely devoted to Mindszenty. He began it startlingly with these words:

" 'A new god has come to you, my people. His fiery eyes do not flash through clouds of incense or from altar candles. They do not gleam from gold-framed darkened pictures of saints. This new god is not a stone statue worn smooth by the kisses of the faithful—he was not born in heaven. He is not far away, nor is he hidden from us. The new god is born from earth and blood—he strides ahead and under the thunder of his steps the globe trembles from East to West. This is the red god. The Seine shudders at his impact and tries to break its banks. Westminster trembles before him like Jericho, and across the green ocean his red shadow falls on the walls of the White House. Hosanna! New God!'

"My dear friends, you know these words are not mine!

THE TRIAL 195

They are the words of an Hungarian Communist, words that echo the thoughts of men depraved and deranged—men who do not know truth, love, justice or faith; men who as their gods know only Satan and Stalin! Yes, these lines come from the pen of a Satan-bred man and are taught to the youth of red-enshackled lands—lands where everybody is afraid of everybody else, where even a son fears his father and fathers fear their own blood-sons, as all become serfs and victims of the relentless god of Baal!

"Yes, the blasphemous lines I have just quoted to you are wild words, but they are wild words of warning and, unless we listen well and realize that we must counteract them by concerted, constant prayer and action, then these words but foretell America's and the whole world's doom."

He then reviewed briefly the story of Mindszenty's torture, and recalled how, when the Cardinal had visited New York, he had said, "My enemies can take from me no more than my life, and that has already been given to God."

Cardinal Spellman then uttered a warning to America. "In our own dear land," he said, "each free man and woman must protect and fight to keep his own integrity of conscience, his own God-given freedoms, and exert every effort to save America and the rest of the democratic, God-loving world from trickery, torturings, disasters, and defeat. For if we fail to learn a lesson from Cardinal Mindszenty's martyrdom, we shall fail ourselves and ourselves face Communist conquest and annihilation. . . . .

"Rebellion to tyrants is obedience to God. . . .

"Are we, the American people, the tools and the fools for which the Communists take us? Are we always to endure the insults and wounds they inflict upon our American honor and decency as they enslave countries and persecute peoples, as they inflict wounds and beatings upon decent, God-loving men and patriots like Cardinal Mindszenty?"

At the Vatican, Pope Pius, sitting upon the Papal throne, solemnly addressed a group of sixteen Cardinals calling the arrest and conviction of Mindszenty "a most serious outrage which inflicts a deep wound not only on your distinguished college and on the church, but also on every upholder of the dignity and liberty of man. The principle object of the trial," he went on, "was to disrupt the Catholic Church in Hungary, and for precisely the purpose set forth in sacred scripture: 'I shall strike the shepherd, and the sheep of the flock shall be dispersed.' Now that things have come to such a pass that this most worthy prelate has been condemned like a criminal we cannot but make a solemn protest."

It was to be expected that the head of the Church should protest. But this was only the beginning. All over Italy there were protest gatherings. In Milan 5,000 Catholics fought bitterly against Communists who tried to break up their meeting. The Italian Government sent a message of "fraternal solidarity" to Hungarian Catholics. In Paris 30,000 people of all faiths and all political beliefs conducted a mass demonstration, and the French Government made an official expression of the nation's "deep emotion." Ernest Bevin in London said, "The trial is utterly repugnant." London's Albert Hall was filled to capacity by over 6,000 Britons, while 25,000 more waited outside in the rain, some kneeling in prayer, and speaker after speaker denounced the Mindszenty trial. One of them cried, "Christ is indeed the Prince of Peace but not of

THE TRIAL 197

peace at any price." In Rio de Janeiro 250,000 people gathered in the streets in protest. The trial was rapidly becoming a boomerang, circling back in the direction of Moscow from which it had been launched.

President Harry S. Truman called the trial "infamous" and said that it had been conducted by a "kangaroo court." Secretary of State Dean Acheson said, "The people of the United States and of all other freedom-loving nations are sickened and horrified." The United States House of Representatives unanimously asked for UN action against Hungary.

There were immediate repercussions in the deterioration in United States-Hungarian relations. Robin Steussy, a secretary in the United States Legation at Budapest, was asked by the Hungarian Government to leave the country. The United States declared John G. Florian, secretary of the Hungarian Embassy, unwelcome. Hungary asked the United States to recall its Minister, Selden Chapin, whom the Reds had accused of conspiring with Mindszenty. Chapin on his way home said, "No one, except the blind and twisted, can fail to see that the Hungarian people are under the total domination of a group of Moscow-trained Communists whose sole allegiance is to the Kremlin." Of Mindszenty he said, "It is impossible to explain the transformation of that lion who was the chief of the Hungarian Catholic Church. He was a great man."

In Washington, New York, Cleveland, nine Hungarian Consular diplomatic officials resigned in protest against the trial. A delegation of New Yorkers carrying a protest to Bela Belassa, acting Hungarian Consul General in New York, were surprised when he greeted them with, "I completely agree with your protests. I am resigning as of this moment." His wife said, "We shall miss the hills of Buda and the plains of Pest, but we have learned to love another country and its liberty."

Before New York's City Hall fifty thousand people gathered, many of them carrying signs condemning the trial and Communism, and many of them kneeling in prayer on the sidewalks.

The prophecy which Mindszenty had made at the moment of his arrest was being demonstrated. The Cardinal, to all intents and purposes, dead, was stirring the conscience of the world as he had been unable to do in the full freedom of his active life.

XVIII
The Picture

THE liquidation of Mindszenty by the Communists has a meaning not only for Hungary and not only for the Catholic Church but for peoples of all faiths throughout the world. Indeed the Communists themselves intended more by it than merely to break the resistance of Hungarian Catholics. It was intended as an example, as conclusive evidence to show what happens to any freedom-loving opponent of Communist rule.

Behind the Iron Curtain the adherents of all religious creeds, Catholics, Protestants, and Jews, are either compelled by their faith to oppose the Communists, or by the Communists to renounce their faith. In Roumania six Greek Catholic Bishops have been forced by the Communist Government to separation from Rome and to complete cooperation with the State. In Czechoslovakia and the western Ukraine, the governing power is trying by every means to bring about the same separation. The persecution of Protestants is less conspicuous only because of their smaller numbers. In Hungary the brave Protestant Bishop Lajos Ordas is also under arrest. Mindszenty is an example set before the people behind the Iron Curtain to help break the resistance of others.

After the trial Joseph Revai, chief spokesman of the

Hungarian Communists, said, "Joseph Mindszenty was brought to trial only after the Vatican had rejected an opportunity to withdraw him. The Vatican was officially informed of all of the charges against him in plenty of time to remove him. When this produced no action, the trial was inevitable."

The Vatican has confirmed the fact that it was so informed and given the opportunity to remove Mindszenty. It is also clear that there were other opportunities for him to escape up to the last minute before his arrest. He could have lived in freedom. In another country of the western world he could have become a hero and a mighty voice in condemnation of the barbarity which had oppressed him and his people.

That Mindszenty, knowing this, made no compromise, that he did not leave Hungary though he knew that the road was opened for him, that he refused to yield to any temptation to come to agreement with his persecutors, can be explained only in one way: he knew that he could still serve the world by living in exile but life outside of Hungary would be only a bare existence in defeat; in death he could perform a higher service to his country and to the world. He knew that he would not be able to withstand the torture chamber and that he would eventually break down and say what they wanted him to say. By this in effect he would tell the world, "See what happens to a strong man behind the Iron Curtain. How much more surely will it happen to the weak." He expected to die and by his death he would say, "This also will happen to you, good men, unless you destroy this menace."

He chose to make a protest which would immediately

THE PICTURE

reverberate in the conscience of the world and ring throughout history. He chose the martyrdom of complete debasement. He chose to show the world the inevitable state of a champion of freedom behind the Iron Curtain. He chose to demonstrate to all of us how even the strongest man becomes putty under the skilled barbarity of Bolshevik tyrants. This he decided was the greatest service he could render.

The torture and murder of Father Salesius Kiss and other martyrs had not been impressive enough to open the eyes of the world. The tragedy of the defendants of the conspiracy trial did not reveal before the world the horrors of the secret police of 60 Andrassy Street and of Soviet jurisdiction. The world had taken little notice of them. It had closed its eyes, not wishing to see, and stopped up its ears, not wishing to hear. Only the martyrdom of Mindszenty could serve as a warning loud enough to be heard everywhere. It was necessary that he be tortured in order that the world might see what happens to a man behind the Iron Curtain. Mindszenty's arrest, his torture, the trial and the photographs, perhaps especially the photographs, have opened the eyes of the world as Mindszenty intended that they should.

Throughout the civilized world, men are asking these questions:

Who are those who do these things which are revealed by the story of Joseph Mindszenty?

Why do honest, righteous men such as Mindszenty, placed on trial in such places as Budapest and Sofia, make such astounding answers to their accusers?

Under what spell do they speak?

What is the drug which transforms them? What breaks their wills?

Throughout the world it has now become known that there is a drug named aktedron which paralyzes the will. The world knows, too, since Mindszenty has stimulated its attention, that defendants are prepared for trial in torture chambers, that air is pumped out of these chambers, that there are special rubber-walled cells, in which beatings are administered which leave no external signs, that there is treatment with electricity, preparation in wet dungeons, beatings administered with diabolical skill, quizzings held without break during several days while the prisoner is kept constantly standing under the light of Jupiter lamps which dazzle the eyes—all of these ghastly facts are now known to millions of people who would not have known them had it not been for Mindszenty's martyrdom.

Two photographs of the martyred Cardinal are now familiar to the world—the one of a face strong and firm in purpose, the Cardinal Mindszenty before the trial, the other, taken of him in the courtroom, a face tortured and dazed, almost the face of a man under hypnosis.

For those whose eyes have not been opened by the Mindszenty trial there is further enlightenment in the words of the chief ideologist of the Hungarian Communist Party, Joseph Revai, who after Cardinal Spellman's magnificent sermon on February sixth, said at a mass-meeting at the sporting-hall of Budapest:

"If the Mr. Spellmans would rather have a dead cardinal we can give them that, too." It was as though he had said plainly: "The court of appeals is still to come; it will deliver the sentence which we order. The shadow of the gal-

THE PICTURE

lows still hovers over Mindszenty's head. Be quiet. Do not demonstrate! Remember that the cardinal is in our hands."

But the world will not be silenced. Mindszenty's picture is before it.

His suffering face revealed in the photographs taken during the trial remains with a clear message for us—the message he wanted to deliver to us: "Do you want the fate of the whole world to be that which has befallen the people behind the Iron Curtain? Shall the face of the world become as the tortured face of Joseph Mindszenty?"

Shall that be the future?

INDEX

Acheson, Dean, 197
Alapi, Gyula, 189, 191
Androssy, Gyula, 52
Apor, Vilmos, 68
Apor, William, 111
Aron, Marton, 110
Arpad, 41
Asztalos, Father, 124 ff.
Attila, 21, 22
Aurelius, Marcus, 21

Balogh, Stephen, 113
Banas, Laszlo, 110, 135
Baranyai, Justin, 182, 183
Baranyai, Lipot, 183
Barcs, Sandor, 173
Bardossy, Laszlo de, 78, 79, 82
Bartok, Bela, 162
Batthanyi, Count, 61, 62
Belassa, Bela, 197
Bevin, Ernest, 196
Bodonyi, Martin, 178
Brennus, 23, 24
Bukarin, 147
Buky, Joseph, 84 ff.

Casanova, 73
Cassius, Dio, 21
Cavallier, Joseph, 162
Chapin, Selden, 188 ff., 197
Charles I, King, 32, 34, 52
Charles IV, King, 44
Charles V, King, 25
Claudius, Tiberius, 21
Constantinus, 21
Csapo, Andrew, 172
Csikos-Nagy, Joseph, 179

Csillery, Andrus, 75
Cziraky, Count, 183

Decsi, Gyula, 169, 170
Dinnyes, Lajos, 130 ff., 139
Diocletian, 21
Dobi, Istvan, 139 ff.

Eckhardt, Tibor, 73, 100
Emma, Sister, 28 ff.
Erdos, Marcus, 37
Esztergalyos, Janos, 61
Eitner brothers, 66 ff.
Eitner, Stephen, 70, 71
Esterhazy, Prince Paul, 170, 171, 182

Fabian, Janos, 173
Faulhaber, Cardinal, 77
Florian, John G., 197
Francis I, King, 25
Frangepan, Count, 12

Gratianus, 21
Gero, Ernest, 136

Hajdu-Nemeth, Mr., 101
Halmos, 91, 92
Hitler, Adolf, 77, 119
Horatius, 23
Horthy, Nicholas, 6, 52, 53, 82, 87, 88
Horvath, Peter, 101

Imre, Prince, 16
Ispanky, Bela, 170, 188

INDEX

Jaszovsky, Joseph, 161

Kallay, Nicholas, 82
Kamenev, 147
Kapisztran, Janos, 26
Karolyi, Michael, 32, 33
Karoly, Ambrus, 159
Kelemen, Chrisostom, 111
Kerkai, Eugen, 88 ff.
Kern, Dr. Aurel, 75, 76, 80
Khan, Ghengis, 118, 119
Kincs, Istvan, 35
Kiczko, Kalman, 181, 191
King of Sweden, 93
Kiss, Father Salesius, 201
Koczan, Father, 172
Kodaly, Zoltan, 162
Kossuth, 41
Kozi-Horvath, Joseph, 176, 186
Kray, Istvan, 183
Kriston, Monsignor, 115
Kun, Bela, 3, 4, 33 ff., 45 ff., 102, 144, 181

Lakatos, General, 87
Lehar, Antal, Baron, 48
Leopold, King, 12
Linder, Bela, 33

Martinuzzi, 159
Matheovics, Ferenc, 141, 142
Megyesi-Schwartz, Robert, 96
Mikes, Janos, 34, 48, 49
Miklos, Bela, 102

Nadashi, Chief Justice, 12
Nagy, Karoly, 146
Nagy, Miklos, 170, 188
Nagy, Vince, 110
Napoleon, 119
Nyisztor, Zoltan, 152

Olti, Vilmos, 178

Ordas, Lajos, 199
Oszko, Gyula, 172
Otto, Archduke, 52, 162, 176, 183, 184, 186, 188, 191

Pallavicini, Marquis, 186
Pazmany, 159
Pehm, Barbara, 31
Peter, Gabor, 172
Peter, Mrs. Janos, 95, 98
Peto, Dr. Erno, 63, 65
Pfeiffer, Zoltan, 109, 110, 137
Pope Pius XII, 153, 196

Rakosi, Mathew, 102, 109 ff., 116, 130, 131, 134, 135, 140
Regulus, 23
Reile, Jacob, 90 ff.
Revai, Joseph, 141, 199, 202
Revesz, Ferenc, 141
Ribbentrop, 77, 78
Riesz, Istvan, 109, 110, 147
Romanelli, Colonel, 42
Roosevelt, Franklin D., 92
Rossler, Sister Gisella, 57 ff.
Rothschild, 35
Ruby, Elizabeth, 57, 69 ff.

Salesius, Father, 120
Scaevola, Mucius, 23
Schlachta, Margit, 183
Schiberna, Dr. Ferenc, 95 ff., 100
Schmidt, Sandor, 179
Schweitzer, Martin, 178
Seredy, Cardinal Prince Primate Justinian, 110, 111
Severus, Alexander, 21
Severus, Septimus, 21
Sigray, Antal, 48
Spellman, Francis Cardinal, 112, 184, 191, 194, 195, 202
Stalin, Josef, 112, 195

INDEX 207

Stephen, St., 15, 16, 43, 44, 111
Steussy, Robin, 197
Stritch, Cardinal, 184
Sulyok, Dezso, 83 ff., 102, 103
Sulyok, Mrs. Dezso, 83
Sviridov, Lieutenant General, 120
Sylvester II, Pope, 15, 16
Szabadhegy, Szabolcs, 96
Szalasi, Ferenc, 88, 175
Szamuelly, Tibor, 33, 46
Szatmari, Jeno, 128
Szecheny, George, 75
Szegfu, Gyula, 162, 168
Szinger, Cornelius, 76
Szollossy, Deputy Prime Minister, 175, 176
Szombathely, Bishop of, 53
Sztojay, Doeme, 82, 87

Tatray, Karoly, 140
Tecsy, Sister Palma, 57 ff.
Teleki, Bela, 66
Teleki, Joseph, 7
Teleki, Paul, 77, 78
Thorez, 73
Tildy, Zoltan, 113, 116, 117
Timar, Colonel, 80, 81
Tomori, Archbishop Stephen, 26
Toth, Laszlo, 170, 189

Truman, Harry S., 197
Tukhachevsky, 147

Ugrin, Archbishop, 26

Valentinianus, 21
Vallus, 21
van Roey, Cardinal, 184
Varga, Bela, 66, 67, 73, 74, 87 ff., 93, 100, 105, 106, 116, 156, 165
Varga, Eugen, 105, 106
Varga, Laszlo, 125
Vazsony, William, 2
Veer, Emery, 152
Vidoczy, Reverend Stephen, 70
Vishinsky, 147
Vitez, John, 159
Voroshilov, Marshal, 112, 113, 119

Wallenberg, Raoul, 92
Weiss, Samuel, 77

Zakar, Andrew, 170, 171, 173, 183 ff.
Zinoviev, 147
Zita, Queen, 184
Zrinyi, Joseph, 29, 36
Zrinyi, Peter, 12
Zsarnay, Kalman, 109